LEARNING THE NEMETH BRAILLE CODE

A Manual for Teachers
and Students

Ruth H. Craig

Adopted by
The Braille Authority of North America
November 1987

Reviewed and updated by the Mathematics Technical Committee

of the BRAILLE AUTHORITY OF NORTH AMERICA

with the permission of Ruth H. Craig

American Printing House for the Blind

Louisville, Kentucky

LEARNING THE NEMETH BRAILLE CODE, A Manual for Teachers and Students, was adopted by the Braille Authority of North America November, 1987.

Grateful acknowledgement is accorded the members of the Mathematics Technical Committee of the Braille Authority of North America: Betty S. Epstein, Von E. Eulert, Christopher Gray, Joyce Van Tuyl, and Ruth H. Craig.

Contents

Preface   v
Foreword to 1986 Revision   vii
Concept of Braille Indicators   1
Numeric Indicator   1
Signs and Symbols of Operation   4
Equals Sign   4
Spatial Arrangements for Computation   5
Fractions   16
Cancellation   21
Punctuation Indicator   26
Omissions   33
Type Forms   35
Alphabets and Alphabetic Indicators   36
Capitalization   40
Abbreviations   41
Signs and Symbols of Grouping   44
Contractions and Short-Form Words   50
Signs and Symbols of Comparison   60
Miscellaneous Signs and Symbols   62
Set Notation   65
Shapes   67
Superscripts and Subscripts   71
Modifiers   75
Radicals   78
Format   79
Cumulative Lists of Rules   82
    Numeric Indicator   82
    Punctuation Indicator   82
    English-Letter Indicator   83
    Contractions   84
    Multipurpose Indicator   85
Answer Section   87
Index   121

Preface

The Nemeth Braille Code for Mathematics and Science Notation, 1972 Revision, published by the American Printing House for the Blind, is a reference work. This manual is a text for learning those parts of the Nemeth Code likely to be used in elementary school, junior high school, and high school mathematics, the levels collectively referred to at several points in the manual as "school mathematics" as distinguished from higher mathematics. It is designed primarily for use in teacher-training programs, but it may also serve to teach the Nemeth Code to new braille readers in upper grades and high school, and even as a self-teaching text for individual teachers.

The unique feature of the manual is that the material is presented sequentially, one group of symbols and applicable rules at a time. Each new symbol and rule is illustrated, and each group of related new rules is followed by practice exercises for the student. No illustration includes symbols or transcription practices which have not yet been explained. Some of the illustrative material is taken directly from *The Nemeth Braille Code for Mathematics and Science Notation, 1972 Revision,* hereafter called the "Code Book," but much of it is new. The self-imposed constraint of using only previously presented symbols and concepts greatly increased the difficulty of composing illustrative examples, but I have tried to present examples that would occur in school mathematics through senior high school.

The sequence of presentation is arbitrary, but I have attempted to move in a reasonable progression, adding units that steadily increase the student's control of mathematical vocabulary in braille. A different sequence would admittedly be possible, but would require a complete revision of the manual. Its sequential construction demands that it be used exactly as written.

The numerical order of rules and sections in the manual is not consecutive. For ease in verifying or expanding information on topics included, rule and section numbers for these topics in the Code Book are used in the manual. However, since much material from the Code Book has been omitted, and what is covered has been rearranged, the rule and section numbers in the manual are out of order.

The choice of symbols and concepts to be included was made after examination of thousands of pages of elementary, junior high, and high school mathematics texts. A teacher using a particular text may encounter an occasional symbol not included in this manual, but if he* has learned to use all the symbols and rules given here, he should have no difficulty in finding the additional material in the Code Book itself and using it successfully.

In writing the manual I have made several assumptions: first, that the user knows Standard English Braille; second, that he has access to a copy of the Code Book; and third, that he is concerned with using braille mathematical texts in teaching, and with transcribing limited mathematics exercises for classroom use, not with transcribing texts.

The need for exactness in use of the Nemeth Code in formal transcription for publication is recognized. In the classroom with blind pupils, time limitations are very real, and the

---

*We recognize that the user of the manual may be male or female, but until we have in our language one pronoun denominating both genders, we will use the masculine. – The Editors.

mathematics teacher on every grade level must be sure that the learning of concepts is not sacrificed to slavish devotion to time-consuming techniques. In this manual I have tried to point out and recommend those symbols and algorithms most readily written by pupils on the brailler. All current published material on the Nemeth Code seems to be written from the point of view of the student of advanced mathematics and the transcriber of his materials. I have tried to think in terms of the much larger body of users of braille mathematics – school-age children and youth. I hope this manual will help their teachers and prospective teachers to learn and use the parts of the Code that they need in their work.

Throughout the manual students are instructed to copy the examples illustrating each new rule before transcribing the practice exercises. This insures that the student's first use of the new material will be correct. It should increase understanding of the rule in question and promote accurate transcription of similar problems.

I wish to express warm gratitude to Ralph McCracken, who years ago saw the handouts I had prepared for my classes and encouraged me to expand them into a book, and has since helped me with many problems; to Alice M. Mann, former head of the mathematics section of the National Braille Association, who has also offered encouragement and interest over the years and who read an earlier version of the manuscript and supplied invaluable suggestions; to Dr. Abraham Nemeth, who cheerfully answered questions on points of difficulty; to Dr. Ouida Fae Morris and her former students at Boston College, who field-tested the manual and sent me detailed questions and comments that led to a number of improvements; and to Dr. Darwin F. Gale, my department chairman, for encouragement and nudging. For unfailing support and for good humor and patience with late meals and dusty furniture I give special thanks to my loyal husband.

Ruth H. Craig
Brigham Young University

Foreword to 1986 Revision

In 1982 the Braille Authority of North America charged the BANA Mathematics Technical Committee "to write an adjunct to the existing mathematics braille code which does not change the code rules but, rather, simplifies the rules to meet the practical needs of teachers and students who learn mathematics through the high school level." In carrying out this task, the committee has investigated several approaches. Most significantly, the creation of a Nemeth Code subset was considered, i.e. the creation of a condensed code which would have been comprised of selected portions of the official Code. After considerable study, this approach was abandoned because of its potential to generate confusion and inaccuracy within the whole Code, the amount of time such a virtual "rewrite" project would take before any results could be realized, and the unnecessary investment of money such a far-ranging project could represent.

It became obvious to the Committee that the true need was for a nontechnical training manual or teacher tutorial. Such a manual should give clear, nontechnical descriptions and real-life examples of the Nemeth Code in day-to-day classroom use.

The Committee examined existing manuals of this nature and selected LEARNING THE NEMETH BRAILLE CODE, a Manual for Teachers, by Ruth H. Craig, Brigham Young University Press, 1979, as an outstanding candidate for this purpose. Craig spent many years training special education teachers in braille, including the Nemeth Code. She developed the manual to fill the need for a text in teaching the Code.

The Committee has reviewed the text and examples thoroughly. Where appropriate, clarifications have been made, examples updated and other changes made. This book conforms in every respect to the Nemeth Code as currently specified by the Braille Authority of North America. It, however, should not be substituted for the Nemeth Code by transcribers of mathematics textbooks as it does not contain all the rules pertinent to textbook transcription.

Particularly, the committee wishes to thank Ruth Craig for her continuous, willing and able assistance with this work and for becoming a committee member in the later stages of the work. The book owes much to her cooperative spirit and to her ability to examine words and phrases in the smallest detail, not to mention the years of work and experience that are embodied within the text. It is hoped that the classroom teacher and the braille-using student will find the book a valuable tool in their general understanding of the Nemeth Code.

Mathematics Technical Committee of
The Braille Authority of North America

Von E. Eulert, Chair
Ruth H. Craig
Betty S. Epstein
Christopher Gray
Joyce Van Tuyl

Rule I – Braille Indicators; Rule II – Numeric Signs and Symbols

Note: The rules of the "Code of Braille Textbook Formats and Techniques, 1977" are followed for the general format in mathematics textbooks but, when special format rules are included in the Nemeth Code, the Nemeth Code rules take precedence.

Rule I – Braille Indicators

§ 5 Concept of Braille Indicators

The limitations of the six-dot cell make it impossible to represent in braille, without duplication, the many arbitrary signs and the various type styles used in print mathematics. A system of braille "indicators" is therefore employed. Like the composition signs of Standard English Braille, the mathematical indicators have no corresponding print signs, but impart particular meanings to the braille symbols which precede or follow them. Their use makes it possible to construct the hundreds of symbols required in modern mathematical and scientific expression.

Rule II – Numeric Signs and Symbols

Note: Throughout the Nemeth Code the word *sign* refers to a character or sequence of characters in print: the word *symbol* refers to a character or sequence of characters in braille. The same practice is followed in this manual. The term *Code Book* refers to *The Nemeth Braille Code for Mathematics and Science Notation, 1972 Revision*, published by the American Printing House for the Blind. *English Braille* refers to the literary code, *English Braille, American Edition*, in contrast to Nemeth Braille.

§ 7 Representation of Arabic Numerals

The familiar "Number Sign" of English Braille is the "Numeric Indicator" in Nemeth Code. Its use differs in the Code in that it is not necessary before every numeral. This is because the digits are represented by the symbols for "a" through "j," but dropped into the lower two-thirds of the braille cell. This placement distinguishes them from letters (provided that the orientation within the cell is clear). The Numeric Indicator is used when there might be a question in the reader's mind as to whether the symbol is in the upper or the lower part of the cell, and in such cases identifies the symbols that follow it as numerals. When there is no likelihood of confusion, the Numeric Indicator is not used. The abbreviation NI will be used in place of the two words from now on in this manual.

The ten digits are shown below with the NI to illustrate their placement in the braille cell:

⠼ ⠁ 1   ⠼ ⠃ 2   ⠼ ⠉ 3   ⠼ ⠙ 4   ⠼ ⠑ 5

⠼ ⠋ 6   ⠼ ⠛ 7   ⠼ ⠓ 8   ⠼ ⠊ 9   ⠼ ⠚ 0

The digits are written this way, in the lower part of the cell, in order that they may be used in conjunction with letters in mathematical expressions such as "2ab" without confusion between the numerals and the letters.

2   **Rule II – Numeric Signs and Symbols**

Use of English Braille Numerals: In works transcribed in the Nemeth Code, English Braille numerals are used for all numerals on title pages and for those indicating page numbers both at the corners of pages and at the end of page-separation lines. They must also be used in the technique of "keying," shown in § 187 of the Code Book. *In all other cases, the numerals of the Nemeth Code must be used.*

§ 9 Use of the Numeric Indicator

The NI must be used before a numeral at the beginning of a braille line or after a space, sometimes called "open" numerals. This avoids confusion as to the reading level within the braille cell.

Numeral at the beginning of a line:

⠼⠢ 5   ⠼⠒⠴ 30   ⠼⠖⠲⠁ 641

Numeral after a space:

⠠⠞⠊⠍ ⠺⠁⠇⠅⠫ ⠼⠒ ⠍⠊⠇⠑⠎⠲ Tim walked 3 miles.

⠠⠺⠑ ⠓⠁⠧⠑ ⠼⠁⠑ ⠃⠕⠭⠑⠎⠲ We have 15 boxes.

The NI is not used before all numeric symbols in all circumstances. Further rules for use, and specific rules for non-use, will be given as needed.

Practice Exercise
Practice writing numerals until the change to the lower position in the cell is comfortable. Write:

0   1   2   3   4   5   6   7   8   9   Repeat several times.
20   13   74   96   58   314   726   509   483   265

§ 12 Long Numerals and the Mathematical Comma

When the comma is used to partition a long numeral into short segments, it is considered a numeric symbol, not a mark of punctuation. Dot 6 represents this comma. No space follows it when it is used within a long numeral. Dot 6 also represents the comma when the comma follows a mathematical symbol as a mark of punctuation. In that case, a space follows the comma. This use is presented and illustrated on page 26 of this manual.

⠼⠃⠠⠢⠴⠶ 2,507   ⠼⠶⠁⠖⠠⠶⠃⠴ 716,920

Why is a comma different from the literary comma necessary?

Rule II – Numeric Signs and Symbols

Division of long numerals: In the Nemeth Code, *a long numeral is never divided and run over to a new line if it can be kept intact by moving all of it to the new line.* This may leave any number of blank cells on the line above the numeral.

⠼⠒ ⠼⠢ ⠼⠢ ⠼⠦ ⠼⠆ ⠼⠢ ⠼⠢ ⠼⠢ ⠼⠢ ⠼⠢ ⠼⠢ They have boxed over

500,000,000,000 screws.

That manufacturer ordered

7,409,683,600 labels last year.

A numeral too long to fit on one braille line must be divided by placing a hyphen after a comma, as in English Braille. The mathematical hyphen is the same as the literary hyphen. In Nemeth Code, unlike English Braille, the NI must be used at the beginning of the new line on which a divided numeral is completed.

Americans consumed 297,556,000,-

000,000,000,000,000 pills

during that period.

Copy the examples above.

§ 8,c The Decimal Point

The decimal point is transcribed in Nemeth Code by dots 4-6 just as in English Braille. It is a numeric symbol when associated with a numeral, subject to the rules for transcribing numerals, and therefore must be preceded by the NI at the beginning of a line or after a space.

⠼⠖⠲⠔⠢ 6.95   ⠼⠦⠲⠲ 8.4   ⠨⠶⠶⠢ .75

⠼⠁ ⠣⠗⠁⠝⠉ ⠊⠎ ⠺⠕⠗⠞⠓ A franc is worth about .20 of a dollar.

Practice Exercise
Write each of these numerals as if following a space:
29.65   524.8   .33   2.7   .001

§ 13 Representation of Numerals to Non-Decimal Bases

Pages 17-18 of the Code Book present several alternatives for representing numerals to bases other than ten when additional digits or symbols different from the standard digits are desired.

Rule XIX – Signs and Symbols of Operation

Following are the most common signs of operation and the Nemeth symbols for them. Except in a few special cases which will be considered later, no space is left either before or after a symbol of operation. Note that no NI is needed between the symbol of operation and the second numeric symbol. Why is this true?

Plus: +   (braille)   (braille) 7 + 3

Minus: −   (braille)   (braille) 41 − 25

Multiplication cross: ×   (braille)   (braille) 6 × 9

Multiplication dot: ·   (braille)   (braille) x·y

Division: ÷   (braille)   "divided by"   (braille) 12 ÷ 3

The two multiplication symbols must not be used interchangeably. The exact symbol used in the print text must be transcribed.

The Equals Sign, =, is a sign of comparison, not a sign of operation, but it is given here so that you may begin writing complete mathematical problems. With this sign, as with other signs of comparison, a space must usually be left on both sides of the symbol. Dots 4-6, 1-3 in two successive cells form this symbol.

(braille) =   (braille) 3 × 10 = 30

Why must the NI be used before 30 in the example above? Copy this example. Recalling the rules for use of the NI with the decimal point, decide where you need the NI in the problem .35 + .50 = .85, and write this problem.

Practice Exercise
Write the following problems and their answers, in the format shown in the examples above. This is "linear" format. Use no letter sign in the last problem.

$11 + 8 =$ $1.00 − .75 =$ $12 × 10 =$ $40 − 5 =$ $49 ÷ 7 =$ $78 + 59 =$
$1.5 × 5 =$ $209 + 62 =$ $.27 ÷ .09 =$ $4 × 7 =$ $n · 6 =$

Dividing problems at the ends of lines should be avoided, but if it is necessary, the division may be made before an equals symbol. No hyphen is used.

Rule II, 9,a Numeric Indicator after Minus Symbol
The NI must be used after a minus symbol which occurs at the beginning of a braille line or after a space.

(braille)   Is −3 more than zero?

Rule XXIV – Spatial Arrangements for Computation

Computation problems are written more often in "spatial" arrangement than in "linear" form. In a spatial arrangement the successive mathematical expressions in the problem are aligned under each other, the answer at the bottom or the top. In the braille transcriptions of addition and subtraction problems shown below, note the following points:

1. In problems arranged spatially for purposes of computation, *the NI is not used.*

2. No line is skipped between rows of numeric symbols.

3. The "separation line" drawn under the arrangement in print is represented in braille by a series of dots 2-5 extending in both directions one cell beyond the overall width of the arrangement. The use of the middle dots of the braille cell leaves wide enough spacing for clarity without skipping a line.

4. Plus and minus symbols are written just above the separation line, in the cell to the left of the widest number above the separation line, regardless of their placement in print.

5. There must be at least one blank cell between the ends of separation lines placed next to each other across the page.

6. One blank line must be left above and below each spatial problem.

Copy all the braille transcriptions above, arranging them according to the rules just given.

6   **Rule XXIV – Spatial Arrangements for Computation**

§ 178,d Carried Numbers in Addition

When carried numbers appear in an addition arrangement above the columns to which they apply, the transcriber must insert a line of dots 2-3-5-6 between these carried numbers and the top line of the problem. This line is called the "carried number indicator." It should have the same length as the other separation line. In the classroom, when "carrying" is being taught, pupils may be reminded to leave line space for the carried numbers and the carried number indicator in setting up every problem. Later, they should learn to carry numbers mentally from one column to the next in order to simplify the task of setting up problems on the brailler.

$$\begin{array}{r} 1 \\ 25 \\ +\ 7 \\ \hline 32 \end{array} \quad \text{Copy this problem.}$$

Practice Exercise

Now transcribe the problems below, including carried numbers when needed. Work the problems directly on the brailler, without using paper and pencil, as blind pupils would need to do.

281	9795	4760	2015	641	209	38	469
$+15$	-8693	$+1483$	$+8392$	-521	5443	67	545
					865	$+42$	$+798$
					$+17$		

In setting up an addition problem of three or more numbers, there is really no need to transcribe the addition sign, since no other operation could be intended.

Spatially arranged problems should never be started near the bottom of one page and run over to the next. The work must be planned so that the problem is completed on one page.

The transcription of the symbols involved in "borrowing" or "renaming numbers" in subtraction will be presented on page 22-23 of this manual.

Rule XXIV – Spatial Arrangements for Computation

§ 179 Spatial Arrangement for Multiplication

In multiplication, the separation line should also extend in both directions one cell beyond the overall width of the arrangement, and in problems with two lines, both should be the same length. Transcribers will adhere scrupulously to this rule, but in the classroom pupils may be allowed some leeway if they fail to estimate correctly the length the lines will need to be. Attempted estimates are good mathematical exercises, however, and should be encouraged.

The multiplication cross is written in the cell next to the first digit of the multiplier, regardless of the length of the multiplicand.

$$230 \times 6 \over 1380$$

$$784 \times 20 \over 15680$$

Zero may be used as a place holder in partial products, just as is sometimes done in print.

$$\begin{array}{r} 123 \\ \times\,54 \\ \hline 492 \\ 615 \\ \hline 6642 \end{array}$$

$$\begin{array}{r} 123 \\ \times\,54 \\ \hline 492 \\ 6150 \\ \hline 6642 \end{array}$$

"Carries" may be indicated in a multiplication problem in the same way as in an addition problem, but the pupil should learn to "carry" mentally as soon as possible.

Practice Exercise

Copy the problems above, then transcribe and compute on the brailler the following:

$$\begin{array}{r} 29 \\ \times\,6 \\ \hline \end{array}$$
$$\begin{array}{r} 6904 \\ \times\,352 \\ \hline \end{array}$$
$$\begin{array}{r} 7240 \\ \times\,83 \\ \hline \end{array}$$
Use zero as a place-holder in this problem.

Rule XXIV – Spatial Arrangements for Computation

In spatially arranged multiplication problems involving decimals, a blank cell should be left in each partial product directly above the decimal point in the final product. This will require the pupil, before beginning to figure the first partial product, to determine the location of the decimal point in the final product by adding the decimal places in the multiplier to those in the multiplicand. A similar procedure must be followed if commas are to appear in the final product, but it is probably easier for pupils in the classroom to work the multiplication problem without commas, and then re-write the answer including commas if that is the final form desired.

Study the examples below, then copy the right-hand one and the lower left-hand one.

$$
\begin{array}{r}
23{,}010 \\
\times\,48 \\
\hline
184\ 080 \\
920\ 40 \\
\hline
1{,}104{,}480
\end{array}
$$

$$
\begin{array}{r}
3010 \\
\times\,48 \\
\hline
24080 \\
12040 \\
\hline
144{,}480
\end{array}
$$

$$
\begin{array}{r}
345.7 \\
\times\,2.77 \\
\hline
24\ 199 \\
241\ 990 \\
691\ 400 \\
\hline
957.589
\end{array}
$$

Rule XXIV – Spatial Arrangements for Computation

§ 180 Division

Many division formats are possible in print: $\overline{)}$; $\underline{|}$; $\overline{|}$; $\underline{|}$; and others.

Only the first format shown above, with division sign on the left and the separation line above, will be used in the following presentation on division. Dots 1-3-5 form this symbol. It is placed in the cell to the left of the dividend. For other division formats and their symbols, see pages 160 and 161, Code Book.

Each separation line in a division problem must begin in the column containing the division symbol and extend one cell to the right of the overall arrangement. The first digit of the quotient is aligned as it would be in print. No NI is used. Copy the examples.

$$\frac{714}{6\overline{)4284}} \qquad\qquad \frac{205}{15\overline{)3075}}$$

Technically, for transcription purposes, a division problem that is stated but does not show the quotient or any partial products should be transcribed in a format entirely different from those shown above; see example 8 on page 172 of the Code Book. However, if problems are being transcribed by a teacher for a pupil to compute, or by the pupil himself, the format shown here is the one needed.

$$\begin{array}{r} 52 \\ 23\overline{)1196} \\ \underline{115} \\ 46 \\ \underline{46} \end{array}$$

Copy this problem.

Practice Exercise

Work these problems on the brailler: $94\overline{)20304}$ $\qquad$ $25\overline{)2575}$ $\qquad$ $375\overline{)802875}$

"Prove" your answer in each case by multiplying the quotient by the divisor. Do both the division and the multiplication directly on the brailler, without using paper and pencil.

10   **Rule XXIV – Spatial Arrangements for Computation**

§ 180, d Division of Decimal Numbers

In formal transcription, when a decimal point occurs in the dividend of a division arrangement, a blank column of cells must be left under the decimal point throughout the arrangement except in separation lines. In the classroom the teacher may want the pupil to place the decimal point in the partial products instead of leaving a space. Some teachers require the pupil to set the decimal point in the correct place in the quotient before he starts computation. Others prefer that the pupil place the decimal point in the quotient whenever he goes to bring down a digit and finds the decimal point instead as the next symbol in the dividend. He may then bring the decimal and the digit that follows it down into the partial product, and repeat the decimal in all succeeding partial products. While this is not proper transcription practice, it may be helpful to pupils just learning to divide decimal numbers.

In dividing decimal numbers, unless the number of decimal places in the solution is specified, it may be impossible for the pupil to know as he starts setting up his problem exactly how far to the right the whole arrangement may extend. Some irregularity in length of separation lines to the right may be allowed.

Here is a problem set up in both ways discussed above. Copy both forms.

$$\begin{array}{r} 2.15 \\ 25\overline{)53.75} \\ \underline{50} \\ 3\,7 \\ \underline{2\,5} \\ 1\,25 \\ \underline{1\,25} \end{array}$$

Practice Exercise

Work the two problems below, omitting decimal points in the first and using them in the second. Prove your answers.

$$68\overline{)215.56} \qquad 42\overline{)59.64}$$

Rule XXIV – Spatial Arrangements for Computation

The caret is used indicate the new position of decimal points moved to facilitate computation in division. The print sign, ^, is represented in Nemeth Braille by dots 4-5-6 in one cell and 1-2-6 in the next:

No spaces are left between this symbol and the numerals associated with it. In transcription of a problem in which a caret occurs in the dividend, throughout the arrangement a blank cell must be left under the original decimal point, and two blank cells under the caret. In the quotient, the decimal point is placed above the second of the two cells used by the caret symbol – it is "right-justified," a printer's term meaning that it is adjusted to the right. Items may be "left-justified" in some situations.

$$\begin{array}{r} 5.2 \\ 1.3\wedge)\overline{6.7\wedge6} \\ \underline{6\ 5} \\ 2\ 6 \\ \underline{2\ 6} \end{array}$$

Observe carefully the spacing in this transcription. Copy it.

    For the pupil performing computation it is simpler to re-write a problem like this, without the caret, and then work it. He must, however, be familiar enough with the caret to understand it when it appears in his mathematics text.

$$2.5)\overline{53.75} \qquad\qquad 25)\overline{537.5}$$

Practice Exercise

Transcribe and solve this problem, using carets: $6.3)\overline{78.75}$

Transcribe this problem, then re-write it for computation without carets: $30.98)\overline{272.5}$

§ 180, f An Alternate Division Arrangement

As you have brailled the long-division problems on pages 9, 10, and 11, you have had to roll your paper up and down a number of times to place a new digit in the quotient, multiply the divisor by it and write the product below, subtract, and bring down the next digit. The pupil may avoid this up-and-down manipulation by using the technique of division by "serial subtraction," or "subtractive method." Students should learn both methods and then be permitted to use whichever seems easier to them for their preferred format. To learn this technique, consult a modern arithmetic text. Copy the braille examples of it below, to compare this style of long division with the standard format for ease of manipulation on the brailler. Another name for this style is the "T-method." Note that a blank cell is left on each side of the vertical line except in separation lines.

```
6) 414  | 10
   60    |
  ----   |
  354    | 20
  120    |
  ----   |
  234    | 30
  180    |
  ----   |
   54    |  9
   54    |
  ----   |
        | 69
```

```
6) 78  | 5
   30  |
  ---  |
   48  | 4
   24  |
  ---  |
   24  | 4
   24  |
  ---  |
    0  | 13
```

Rule XXIV – Spatial Arrangements for Computation

The pupil must be taught to determine spacing needs in advance, or he will not get his partial quotients in the correct columns and will have the wrong answer when he has added them. Notice the spacing of the quotient numbers especially in the second problem on the previous page, where none of the partial quotients require two cells but the final quotient does. The pupil must estimate this need correctly in order to have his partial quotients in the proper place value columns.

Please note that in the examples of division by serial subtraction in the Code Book, on pages 175, 176, the partial quotients are aligned differently. Follow the print placement in the text being used in the classroom or being transcribed.

Problems in long division involving decimals may also be done by repeated subtraction. In such problems, the correct number of zeros for the number of places to which the quotient is to be carried must be included when the problem is first set up, and they must be used in the partial products. Spaces must be left under the original decimal point of the dividend throughout the arrangement, as in the division problems involving decimals that you have already transcribed, or the decimal point may be carried down through the problem if the teacher wishes. The same procedure, whichever one is chosen, should also be followed in the columns of the partial quotients, so that the decimal point will be correctly located in the final quotient.

It is important to realize that students doing division problems involving decimals should determine the placement of the decimal by mathematical reasoning, not by counting places. That is, the answer should be estimated at the beginning of the problem and the position of the decimal point in the quotient will then be understood from the start. In the example shown on page 14, if the student estimates as he starts his computation that the answer will be 1 plus a decimal part, he can place the decimal point correctly in his first trial quotient, carry it down or keep it in mind as he works, and place it correctly in the final quotient with no difficulty.

Study the example on page 14. Notice again the importance of correct placement of the numerals of the partial quotients. Careless placement could easily result in an addition arrangement like the one below left, instead of the correct one, right.

1.000		1.000
800		800
10		10
8		8

To prevent this, the teacher may have the pupil write the decimal point each time, followed by zeros to fill in the empty place values:

| 1.000 |
| .800 |
| .010 |
| .008 |

Here is an example of a long-division decimal problem done by the "subtractive method":

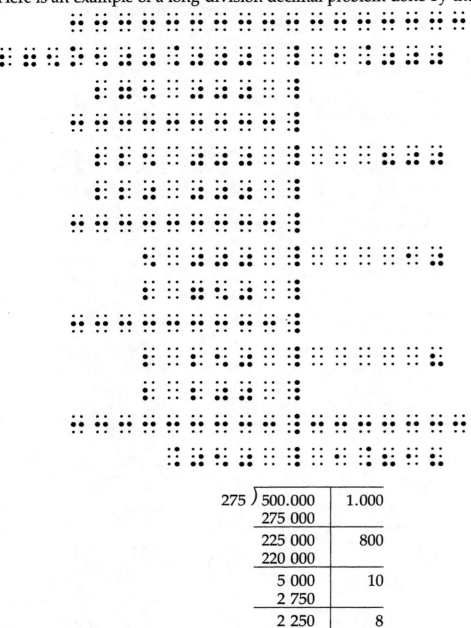

Practice Exercise
Transcribe the problem above, but use the decimal point throughout, and zeros as placeholders.

Rule XXIV – Spatial Arrangements for Computation

§ 180, e Remainders

The remainder in a division problem is often written after the letter *r* on the line with the quotient. In braille the *r* may be lower case or capitalized, as it appears in print, but it must be preceded by a space and followed by dot 5, the "Multipurpose Indicator." You will learn more about the Multipurpose Indicator later. Without it, in this circumstance, the numeral following *r* would be a subscript.

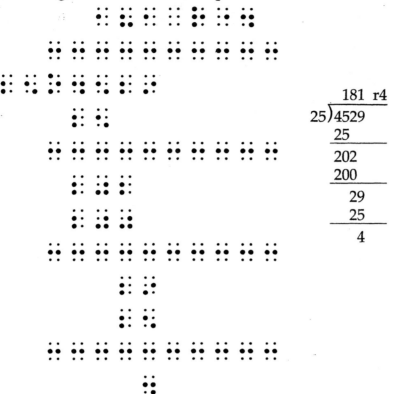

```
        181 r4
    25)4529
       25
       ___
       202
       200
       ___
        29
        25
        __
         4
```

Practice Exercise

Study this example, then transcribe the same problem using the "repeated subtraction" technique. State the remainder as part of the final quotient at the bottom of the arrangement.

If pupils were given a problem like this and did not realize that there would be a remainder, they would not have made the separation lines long enough to extend under and beyond the remainder. What would you require of them in such a case?

Rule XII – Fractions and Fraction Indicators

Fractions may be expressed in print in several ways: $\frac{1}{4}$, ¼, 1/4, for example. For each print style of representation there is an equivalent in Nemeth Code. In this manual only one form – that with the horizontal line – will be presented. The braille fraction lines and fraction indicators change as the print form of the fraction changes, so study Rule XII in the Code Book before trying to write any fractions in forms other than the one presented here. The fraction line is a sign of operation. Spacing follows the usual rules for such signs.

Fractions are usually written in spatial arrangement in print. In braille, they are easier to write and to read in linear form, and this is the preferred method except as indicated in Section 70, page 18, first paragraph, in this manual.

§ 61 Simple Fractions

A simple fraction is one whose numerator and denominator contain no fractions, except possibly as subscripts or superscripts, which are presented later in this manual.

$$\frac{1}{3} \qquad \frac{2 + 3}{6} \qquad \frac{12}{4 \times 5} \qquad \frac{a + b}{c}$$

Horizontal line for simple fractions: ⠌

§ 62 Simple-Fraction Indicators

Simple-Fraction Indicators, ⠹ ⠼ are used to enclose a simple fraction in which the print fraction line is horizontal.

$$\frac{1}{3} \qquad \frac{2 + 3}{6} \qquad \frac{12}{4 \times 5}$$

Why is there no NI in these examples?

Practice Exercise
Transcribe these fractions:

$$\frac{7}{8} \qquad \frac{15}{32} \qquad \frac{3 \times 5}{9}$$

Rule XII – Fractions and Fraction Indicators   **17**

§ 64 Mixed Numbers

A mixed number is an expression consisting of a numeral followed by a simple fraction whose numerator and denominator are both numerals. If the expression contains a letter, as in $n\frac{1}{2}$ or $5\frac{x}{3}$, it is not a mixed number. Remember that we are considering here only those mixed numbers in which the fraction line is horizontal.

The Mixed-Number Indicators, ⠿ ⠿ ⠿ ⠿ ⠿ ⠿ ⠿ not the simple-fraction indicators, must be used to enclose the fractional part of a mixed number.

⠿ ⠿ ⠿ ⠿ ⠿ ⠿ ⠿ ⠿ ⠿ $4\frac{3}{8}$

Practice Exercise
Transcribe these mixed numbers: $16\frac{4}{5}$ $2\frac{2}{3}$ $7\frac{5}{6}$ $10\frac{1}{2}$

§ 65 Complex Fractions

A complex fraction is one whose numerator or denominator, or both, contains at least one simple fraction other than at the subscript or superscript level.

Horizontal line for complex fractions: ⠿ ⠿

§ 66 Complex-Fraction Indicators

Complex-Fraction Indicators, ⠿ ⠿ ⠿ ⠿ ⠿ ⠿ ⠿ must be used to enclose a complex fraction.

⠿ ⠿ ⠿ ⠿ ⠿ ⠿ ⠿ ⠿ ⠿ ⠿ ⠿ ⠿ $\dfrac{\frac{3}{8}}{5}$

⠿ ⠿ ⠿ ⠿ ⠿ ⠿ ⠿ ⠿ ⠿ ⠿ ⠿ ⠿ $\dfrac{6}{\frac{7}{9}}$

⠿ ⠿ ⠿ ⠿ ⠿ ⠿ ⠿ ⠿ ⠿ ⠿ ⠿ ⠿ ⠿ ⠿ ⠿ ⠿ $\dfrac{14\frac{3}{4}}{20}$

⠿ ⠿ ⠿ ⠿ ⠿ ⠿ ⠿ ⠿ ⠿ ⠿ ⠿ ⠿ ⠿ ⠿ ⠿ $\dfrac{\frac{2}{3}}{\frac{5}{8}}$

Practice Exercise
Study the examples above. Then transcribe:

$$\dfrac{3}{\frac{4}{5}} \qquad \dfrac{\frac{1}{3}}{10} \qquad \dfrac{3\frac{1}{2}}{\frac{3}{8}} \qquad \dfrac{4\frac{1}{3}}{6\frac{2}{5}} \qquad \dfrac{\frac{7}{10}}{\frac{9}{15}}$$

Do not forget the closing indicator, either in the inner fraction, or at the end of the whole expression. This is a common mistake.

If it is necessary to move to a new line in the middle of writing a fraction, the division should be made before a fraction line. No hyphen is used. Such divisions should be avoided.

§ 70 Spatial Arrangement for Fractions

When fractions are first introduced in the elementary school, and usually through the lower grades, it is recommended that they be represented spatially for the blind child, as they are for sighted children. The blind child can better understand the principle of "invert and multiply" if he has worked with fractions arranged spatially. Spatial arrangement may be used at any other time when there is special need. Ordinarily, the linear arrangement of fractions should be used.

In spatial arrangements of fractions, the horizontal fraction line is a line of dots 2-5 the same length as the longest expression above or below it. The appropriate fraction indicators are placed at either end of the fraction line, and the terms of the fraction must be centered on the line. *The NI is required* where a numeral would otherwise follow a space in a fraction arranged spatially.

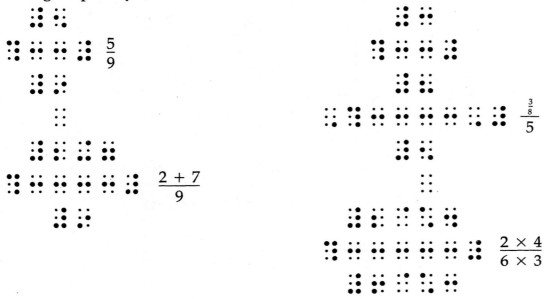

Compare the complexity of these spatial arrangements with that of the linear arrangements of the same fractions below:

Practice Exercise

Copy the spatial arrangements of the fractions above, and then transcribe the following one in both linear and spatial arrangement:

$$\frac{\frac{1+3}{4+5}}{\frac{3+4}{5+6}}$$

Rule XXIV – Spatial Arrangements for Computation

§ 178, e Addition and Subtraction Involving Fractions

In addition and subtraction that involves fractions, the fractions themselves are written in linear form, with the total problem arranged spatially. Fraction lines must be vertically aligned, each numerator must be right-justified – a term explained on page 11 – in the column reserved for numerators, and each denominator must be left-justified in the column reserved for denominators. Fraction indicators must also be vertically aligned, right-justified in the columns reserved for both opening and closing indicators. The plus or minus symbols are placed as in other addition and subtraction problems.

Copy these two examples, planning carefully for the extra spaces needed and for placement of the numerator and denominator symbols.

§ 178, f Arrangements Containing Mixed Numbers

Study the alignment of the fraction indicators and the mixed-number indicators in the arrangements below. Notice that the digits of the whole number parts of the second example are aligned according to place value. Since these are problems arranged for computation, the NI is not used except in the final statement of the answer in the second example. Why is it used there?

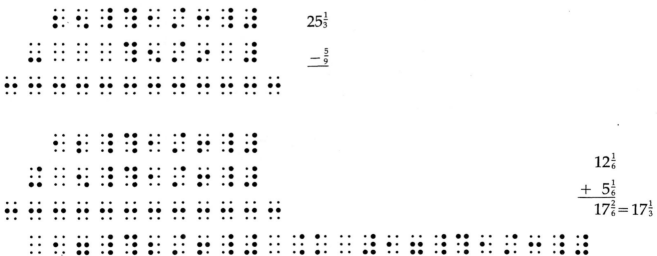

Rule XXIV – Spatial Arrangements for Computation

The following is a good example of spatial arrangement of an addition problem involving mixed numbers and simple fractions. It would require careful planning to achieve correct spacing in transcription, and a good estimate of the answer, in addition to planning of spacing for the pupil computing it on the brailler.

$$5\tfrac{4}{5} = 5\tfrac{8}{10}$$

$$\tfrac{9}{10} = \tfrac{9}{10}$$

$$+4\tfrac{1}{2} = 4\tfrac{5}{10}$$

$$11\tfrac{2}{10}$$

Copy this example. To avoid mistakes:
1. Note the 10 in the denominator in the second line, and as you write the *first* line, allow for the two cells the 10 will require.

2. Estimate the sum of the fractions to be more than the whole number 2, and add that to the whole numbers 4 and 5, so that you know the answer will be 11 plus a fraction.

3. Allow two cells for the 11 in the answer so that you can begin the separation line in the correct cell.

In addition problems, if the order of the individual fraction or mixed numbers is not important, placing the quantity with the largest numerator and denominator first makes spacing easier in writing the remaining ones. (Note how this would help in the second problem on page 19, and in the one above.)

Rule XI – Cancellation

§ 60 The Cancellation Indicators

The Cancellation Indicators, ⠿ ⠿ ⠿ ⠿ ⠿ are used in some types of problems in spatial arrangements, to show the extent of a mathematical expression which has been cancelled in print. A few typical uses are given here.

The cancellation indicators are used in "reducing" fractions. Note that in the reduction of fractions by cancellation, as in any spatial arrangement of fractions, the NI is used before numerals preceded by a space. This kind of problem is not considered work arranged for computation.

$$\frac{6}{36} = \frac{\overset{1}{\cancel{6}}}{\underset{6}{\cancel{36}}} = \frac{1}{6}$$

The portion of such a problem which is not actually involved in the cancellation may be written in linear form. The final step of the problem above, for example, could be written:

$$= \frac{1}{6}$$

A pupil must be able to read the problems using cancellation indicators, but in the classroom he may often save time and avoid the spacing problems which these indicators create by using, at the teacher's or his own discretion, one of several other possible techniques. Mental arithmetic, for example, may shorten the problem above to:

$$\frac{6}{36} = \frac{1}{6}$$

Copy this transcription and the one at the top of the page.

If the teacher wants the cancellation shown more explicitly but with minimum manipulation of the brailler, the same problem might be represented by the pupil in this way:

$$\frac{\overset{1}{\cancel{6}}}{\underset{6}{\cancel{36}}} = \frac{1}{6}$$

In reducing more complicated fractions, renaming the fractions in successive steps is simpler than setting up the problem with cancellation indicators:

$$\frac{16}{128} = \frac{4}{32} = \frac{1}{8}$$

Copy these two problems.

The cancellation indicators are also used in subtraction problems involving "borrowing" or "changing number form" or "regrouping." These would be problems arranged for purposes of computation, and the NI would therefore not be required. Spacing must allow for the insertion of the necessary cancellation indicators and when one item is cancelled at a time, each item must be shown cancelled individually in the transcription.

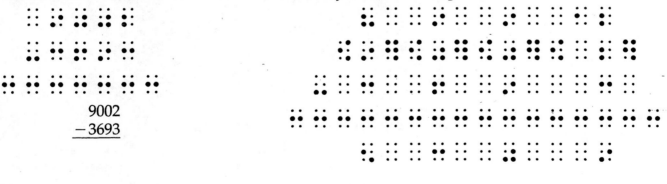

$$\begin{array}{r} 9002 \\ -3693 \\ \hline \end{array}$$

$$\begin{array}{r} 8\;9\;9\;12 \\ \cancel{9}\;\cancel{0}\;\cancel{0}\;\cancel{2} \\ -3\;6\;9\;\;3 \\ \hline 5\;3\;0\;\;9 \end{array}$$

Copy these transcriptions.

Rule XI – Cancellation

The previous example is an illustration of a problem which is as great a challenge to manual dexterity as to mathematical reasoning. Subtraction as currently taught, however, often eliminates the technique of "cancellation." The pupil achieves a larger number at the top of each column in a subtraction problem by using "expanded notation" and "renaming" of numbers. In braille, this process does not save space, but simplifies the difficulties encountered in using the cancellation indicators while promoting good mathematical understanding.

$$
\begin{array}{rcrcr}
72 & = & 70+2 & = & 60+12 \\
-45 & = & -40+5 & = & -40+5 \\
\hline
& & & & 20+7=27
\end{array}
$$

Parentheses may be used around the expanded quantities. These will be presented on pages 44-47 of this manual.

Practice Exercise
A three-digit subtraction problem may be solved by the process just illustrated, adding one additional step. Work this problem on the brailler using expanded notation.

$$
\begin{array}{r}
564 \\
-488 \\
\hline
\end{array}
$$

After pupils learn the subtraction concepts through expanded notation and renaming, they can understand the mental processes involved in the short familiar form and complete a subtraction problem without cancellation indicators, doing the renaming mentally. Especially for blind pupils, this is an important goal to reach. (Pupils should also be learning to use the Cranmer Abacus, calculator or personal computer for most of their computation.)

In addition or subtraction of mixed numbers, cancellation indicators may be needed:

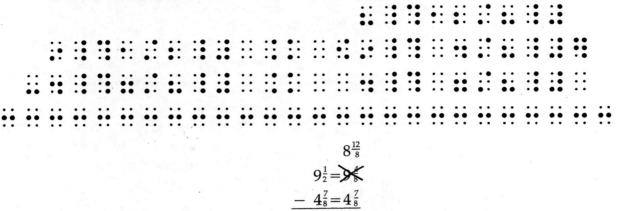

Note the 12 in the numerator in the second part of the arrangement, and allow for it in the lines underneath.

The entire mixed number is cancelled in print and can therefore be enclosed within cancellation indicators in braille.

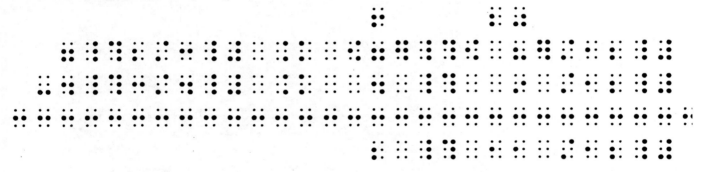

Note the 20 in the numerator, and remember that allowance must be made for it in the lines underneath. The whole number and numerator of the fraction are cancelled separately in print, and therefore are enclosed separately within cancellation indicators.

Rule XI – Cancellation

In classroom situations, as opposed to transcription, it is simpler for the blind student to rewrite the fractions, renaming them so that there is no need for cancellation indicators. The previous example would then appear as follows:

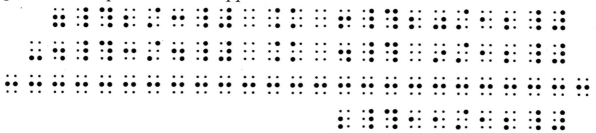

$$7\tfrac{2}{3} = 6\tfrac{20}{12}$$
$$-4\tfrac{3}{4} = 4\tfrac{9}{12}$$
$$\overline{\phantom{-4\tfrac{3}{4} =\;} 2\tfrac{11}{12}}$$

Some students might need three steps for this problem at least when first learning the process:

$$7\tfrac{2}{3} = 7\tfrac{8}{12} = 6\tfrac{20}{12}$$
$$-4\tfrac{3}{4} = 4\tfrac{9}{12} = 4\tfrac{9}{12}$$

Practice Exercise

Transcribe the problem above showing all three steps.

Now transcribe and solve this problem, showing all the steps you would teach to a blind pupil. Do not use cancellation indicators.

$$5\tfrac{4}{5}$$
$$8\tfrac{1}{2}$$
$$+3\tfrac{3}{5}$$

Rule VI – Punctuation Signs and Symbols

§ 37 The Punctuation Indicator

Up to this point you have worked primarily with numeric symbols. In order to read or transcribe explanatory material and story problems, you must know how to combine literary sentences and mathematical expressions. Since the Code numerals, written in the lower part of the cell, are identical in form to the common marks of punctuation, something is often needed to insure distinction between the two. The Punctuation Indicator, dots 4-5-6 serves the purpose of making marks of punctuation distinct from numerals. It is not required with every symbol of punctuation, but when used it identifies the symbol which follows it as a mark of punctuation. *It is generally needed before a literary mark of punctuation that follows a mathematical term or indicator.* Some common instances of its use and non-use are presented here. The abbreviation *PI* will be used for this indicator.

The PI must be used before a mark of punctuation in the following circumstances:

1. After any braille indicator.

⠀⠀⠀⠀⠀⠀⠀⠀⠀⠀⠀⠀⠀⠀⠀⠀⠀⠀⠀⠀⠀⠀⠀⠀⠀⠀

Simplify the fractions $\dfrac{9}{24}, \dfrac{6}{16}$.

The comma in this example illustrates the use of the mathematical comma, dot 6, after a mathematical expression. A space follows it except when it ends the line and when it is used to divide a long number into segments.

2. After any numeric symbol written as in the Nemeth Code.

⠀⠀⠀⠀⠀⠀⠀⠀⠀⠀⠀⠀⠀⠀⠀⠀

Add 7 and 5.

Without the PI, what would this say?

⠀⠀⠀⠀⠀⠀⠀⠀⠀⠀⠀⠀⠀⠀⠀⠀⠀

Does $7 = 4 + 3$?

3. After a Roman numeral.

⠀⠀⠀⠀⠀⠀⠀⠀⠀⠀⠀⠀⠀⠀⠀⠀⠀⠀⠀⠀⠀⠀⠀

Write the Arabic numerals for XXVI.

Rule VI – Punctuation Signs and Symbols

Note. If you use a braille line of different length than is shown here when you copy these examples and those on subsequent pages, or when you transcribe the practice exercises, you should realize that certain mathematical groupings must be kept on one line if possible, and if division is essential, the grouping must be divided only at certain points. Some rules for division have already been given and others will be included at appropriate points through the remainder of the manual. A summary of rules for runovers is presented on pages 80 and 81, and all the illustrative examples throughout the manual follow those rules.

It will help you to understand line divisions in the examples if you will turn now to page 80 and read rule 1 and its illustration, and then rule 5, ii, iii, and iv on page 81. The other rules on those pages include concepts which you have not yet learned.

4. After a dash or ellipsis in mathematical context.

⠿⠿⠿⠿⠿⠿⠿⠿⠿⠿⠿⠿⠿⠿⠿⠿⠿ $5 \times 16 = \underline{\quad}$.

(Note that this calls for the long dash.)

⠿⠿⠿⠿⠿⠿⠿⠿⠿⠿⠿⠿⠿⠿⠿⠿⠿⠿⠿⠿⠿⠿⠿⠿⠿⠿

Odd numbers 1, 3, ...

5. After a sequence of letters, each of which has a separate identity. This category does not include abbreviations.

⠿⠿⠿⠿   ⠿   ⠿⠿⠿⠿⠿   ⠿⠿   ⠿⠿⠿⠿⠿   ⠿   ⠿⠿⠿⠿⠿

Find the value of the combination of xyz.

6. After ordinal endings which are joined to numerals, letters, or other mathematical expressions.

⠿⠿⠿⠿⠿⠿⠿⠿⠿⠿⠿⠿⠿⠿⠿⠿⠿⠿⠿⠿   Mark the 2nd and 4th.

Neither the *th* nor the *st* contraction is used in ordinal endings in the Nemeth Code. Other rules concerning use of contractions begin on page 50.

7. After a plural or possessive ending joined to a mathematical expression, with or without an apostrophe. (The PI is also needed *before* the apostrophe when used in such endings. If the apostrophe is omitted in print, is is also omitted in braille.)

⠿⠿⠿⠿⠿⠿⠿⠿⠿⠿⠿⠿⠿⠿⠿⠿⠿   Include the 0's.

⠿⠿⠿⠿⠿⠿⠿⠿⠿⠿⠿⠿⠿⠿⠿⠿⠿⠿⠿⠿⠿⠿   1's, 2's, and 3's.

⠿⠿⠿⠿⠿⠿⠿⠿⠿⠿⠿⠿⠿⠿⠿⠿⠿   1s, 2s, and 3s.

Copy the examples above.

28 **Rule VI – Punctuation Signs and Symbols**

8. The PI must be used before a mark of punctuation after any abbreviated function name, or unabbreviated function name in mathematical context – both unusual circumstances. Function names and their abbreviations include: sine, sin; cosine, cos; tangent, tan; logarithm, log; etc.

The abbreviation for logarithm is log.

If two or more marks of punctuation follow a mathematical term, only one PI is needed for the sequence.

"Show me the even numbers 2-10."

Copy the two examples above.

Summary of Rules on Use of the Punctuation Indicator
Use the PI before a mark of punctuation that follows:

1. a braille indicator;
2. a Nemeth numeral;
3. a Roman numeral;
4. a dash or ellipsis in mathematical context;
5. a sequence of letters each having separate identity;
6. an ordinal ending joined to a mathematical expression;
7. a plural or possessive ending joined to a mathematical expression;
8. an abbreviated function name, or an unabbreviated one in mathematical context.

Use only one PI before a sequence of punctuation marks.

Practice Exercise
Note. From now on, the problems in each set of practice exercises will be numbered. See Code Book, page 193, § 191 a, i, for correct transcription format.
Transcribe the following:

1. In Roman numerals, 2000 = MM.
2. Underline the prime number: 51, 67, 75, 92.
3. What is the area of the ranch marked "The Lazy 8"?
4. The algebraic product of these variables may be written as grs.
5. Write the next four numbers in the sequence 12, 5, 13, 6, 14, 7, ...
6. The relationship of cosine and secant is expressed as $\frac{1}{\cos}$ = sec.
7. Express as a percent the fraction $\frac{4}{5}$.

Rule VI – Punctuation Signs and Symbols

§ 38 Non-Use of the PI

The PI must NOT be used:

1. Before a mark of punctuation that occurs at the beginning of a braille line or after a space.

Count like this: "3, 6, 9, 12."

Estimate the total for '85.

Note the placement of the apostrophe in this example. It always *precedes* the NI in the Nemeth Code.

2. After any numeric symbol written in English Braille, as on a title page.

Copyright 1970.

3. After a dash or ellipsis in literary context – one that replaces a word.

This Venn diagram illustrates the operation ____.

Five and three are ....

4. After a word or abbreviation. (See § 37, x, Code Book, page 44, for one rare exception.)

e.g.   Find the LCD.

Study pages 23-30.

How many kilometers are there in 50 miles?

Copy the examples on this page.

30 Rule VI – Punctuation Signs and Symbols

5. *Before* a comma, hyphen, dash, or ellipsis.

⠿ ⠿ ⠿ ⠿ ⠿ ⠿ ⠿ ⠿ ⠿ ⠿ 0, 1, 2

⠿ ⠿

5-, 10-, and 15-cent stamps.

⠿ ⠿

⠿ ⠿ ⠿ ⠿ ⠿ ⠿ Five-, ten-, and fifteen-cent stamps.

Note the use of different commas in the two examples above. The mathematical comma is used after mathematical expressions, the literary comma in other cases. The PI is not used before either type of comma.

⠿ ⠿ ⠿ ⠿ ⠿ ⠿ ⠿ ⠿ ⠿ ⠿ ⠿ ⠿ ⠿ ⠿ ⠿ Score: 27—14

⠿ 7, 9, 11, ..., 21

Copy the examples above.

Summary of Rules on Non-Use of the Punctuation Indicator

Do NOT use the PI:
1. before punctuation at the beginning of a braille line or after a space;
2. after an English braille numeral;
3. after a dash or ellipsis that replaces a word;
4. after a word or abbreviation;
5. before a comma, hyphen, dash, or ellipsis.

Practice Exercise

Transcribe the following examples:

1. Measure the distance between Grand Ave. and the bus terminal.
2. The part of a fraction below, or following, the fraction line is called the _____.
3. In '76 the United States was 200 years old.
4. Use a 2-shafted arrow.
5. Can you divide 21 in 4 equal parts?
6. 3, 6, 9, ..., 27.
7. 2 p.m.

Rule VI – Punctuation Signs and Symbols

§ 42, 43 Spacing with Long Dash and Ellipsis

The long dash — not the literary dash – is preceded and followed by a space except when next to symbols of punctuation other than the hyphen or next to braille indicators or other symbols which apply to it. See previous examples under 3 and 5, § 38, and this one:

⠄⠄ ⠠⠄ ⠄⠄ ⠄⠠ ⠄⠠ ⠄⠠ ⠄⠄ ⠄⠄ ⠠⠄ ⠠⠠ ⠠⠄ ⠄⠄ ⠄⠠ ⠄⠠ ⠄⠄ ⠄⠄ ⠠⠄ ⠠⠄ ⠄⠄ ⠄⠄ ⠄⠄ ⠄⠠ ⠠⠠ ⠠⠄ ⠄⠄

A _____ equals five cents.

The above rule applies even if the dash or ellipsis replaces a numeric symbol next to a symbol of operation.

⠄⠄ ⠠⠠ ⠄⠄ ⠄⠄ ⠄⠠ ⠄⠄ ⠄⠠ ⠠⠠ ⠠⠄ ⠄⠄ ⠄⠠ ⠄⠠ ⠄⠄ ⠄⠠ ⠄⠠ ⠄⠄ ⠠⠄ ⠠⠄ $6 = 42 \div \ldots$

Other less common exceptions to this spacing rule are given in § 42, and 43, b, pages 49-51, Code Book.

Copy the examples above.

Practice Exercise
Transcribe these problems:

1. 90 inches = _____ yards.

2. _____ = .75

3. 12 + 4 × _____ = 48

4. $\frac{..}{8} + \frac{1}{4} = \frac{5}{8}$

§ 45 Space between Hyphen and Adjacent Dash

A space must be left between a hyphen and an adjacent dash.

⠄⠄ ⠄⠠ ⠄⠄ ⠠⠠ ⠠⠄ ⠄⠄ ⠠⠄ ⠄⠠ ⠄⠄ ⠠⠠ ⠠⠠ ⠠⠄ ⠄⠄ ⠄⠄ ⠄⠠ ⠄⠠ ⠄⠄ ⠄⠄ ⠄⠄ ⠄⠄ ⠄⠄ ⠄⠄ ⠄⠄ ⠄⠠ ⠠⠄ ⠠⠄ ⠠⠠

⠄⠄ ⠄⠠ ⠠⠠ ⠄⠄ ⠠⠄ ⠄⠠ ⠠⠄   A triangle is a _____ -sided figure.

Copy this example.

Rule II, § 9,b The Numeric Indicator and Punctuation

The NI must be used before a numeric symbol that follows a mark of punctuation.

⠄⠄ ⠄⠠ ⠄⠄ ⠠⠠ ⠄⠄ ⠄⠄ ⠠⠄   2:25

⠄⠄ ⠠⠄ ⠠⠠ ⠄⠠ ⠄⠄ ⠄⠄ ⠄⠠ ⠠⠠ ⠄⠄ ⠄⠠ ⠄⠠ ⠄⠄ ⠄⠠ ⠄⠄   Probability — 0

⠄⠄ ⠠⠠ ⠄⠠ ⠄⠄ ⠠⠠ ⠠⠄ ⠄⠄ ⠠⠠ ⠄⠄ ⠄⠠ ⠄⠄ ⠄⠠ ⠄⠠ ⠠⠠ ⠄⠄ ⠄⠄ ⠄⠄ ⠄⠄ ⠄⠠ ⠄⠄ ⠄⠠ ⠠⠄ ⠠⠄

He read: "5 × 4 = 20."

Rule II, § 9,f and 11,d The Numeric Indicator and the Hyphen

The NI must be used after a hyphen that follows a word, an abbreviation, or a mark of punctuation; but not after a hyphen that follows a mathematical expression.

⠰⠆ ⠲⠄ ⠆⠒ ⠆⠶ ⠆⠶ ⠰⠆ ⠰⠶ ⠲⠒ ⠲⠒ ⠲⠒ ⠲⠶ ⠲⠶ ⠲⠲   carbon-14 dating

⠲⠒ ⠲⠒ ⠲⠆ ⠲⠒ ⠲⠶ ⠲⠶ ⠲⠲   DC-7

⠲⠒ ⠲⠶ ⠲⠒ ⠰⠶ ⠲⠶ ⠲⠶ ⠲⠶ ⠲⠶ ⠲⠶ ⠲⠒ ⠲⠶ ⠲⠶ ⠲⠲   5:45-7:45

Copy the examples above and the last three on page 31.

Practice Exercise

Transcribe the following, reviewing the summaries and pages 26-32 as necessary:

1. Tom said, "7 + 3 − 4 = 5." Do you agree?

2. Read Rules II and IV.

3. List all the possible factors of 48.

4. How many 5's?

5. Convert these fractions to percents: $\frac{2}{5}, \frac{1}{3}, \frac{3}{4}.$

6. When two sets have some, but not all, members in common, we say they _____.

7. Are the hands of the clock at 8:50?

8. Prime numbers between 1 and 10 include 1, 3, ...

9. Jerry worked a _____ -hour shift yesterday.

10. Is the empty set the same as 0?

11. Write the inverse of $\frac{1}{3}.$

12. The Lazy-8 Ranch

13. 7:45-8:15 = _____ minutes?

14. At 8:15 EST, it is _____ CST.

15. 1 + 2 + ... + 7

16. Solve all odd-numbered problems, 1st-15th.

17. Define log.

18. hydrogen-3

19. Can the value of this progression be represented by the sequence aceg?

Rule X – Omissions

§ 57 The General Omission Symbol

Omitted mathematical or literary material may be indicated in many ways in print: by a blank space, dash, ellipsis, question mark, geometric shape as "place holder," dots, etc. In Nemeth braille the "general omission symbol," formed by the full cell, ⠿ , is used to denote omission when the print copy uses a blank space or a question mark either by itself or in combination with hyphens or dashes. The number of general omission symbols used must be the same as the number of omission signs in print, but a question mark combined with hyphens or a dash counts as one sign. The general omission symbol is spaced just as the material it replaces would be spaced.

$? + ? = 10$

$7 - \underline{?} = 5$

$5 \times 25 =$

$7 \times 2\,?\,14$

$9 - 5 = -?-$

$36\,?\,9 = 4$

A PI must be used before a punctuation mark that follows the general omission symbol.

The sum of 23 and 37 is -?-.

As already shown on page 27, when a dash is used for omission in print, the long dash should be used in braille. A braille ellipsis replaces a print ellipsis.

five $\times$ _____ $=$ fifty

$2, 4, 6, \ldots, 10$

Copy the examples on this page.

34   **Rule X – Omissions**

§ 58 Omissions in Work Arranged Spatially for Computation

In work arranged spatially for computation, only the general omission symbol may be used in braille regardless of how the omission is denoted in print. The number of general omission symbols used must be the same as the number of print omission signs.

$$
\begin{array}{r}
40 \\
+\ 70 \\
\hline
??? \\
\end{array}
\qquad\qquad
\begin{array}{r}
572 \\
-\ 304 \\
\hline
? \\
\end{array}
\qquad\qquad
\begin{array}{r}
651 \\
\times\ 252 \\
\hline
\ldots2 \\
\ldots5 \\
\ldots2 \\
\ldots\ldots2 \\
\end{array}
$$

Except for the uses just given for the general omission symbol, the dash and the ellipsis, the specific symbols which the Nemeth Code provides for other print signs of omission must be used in formal transcription. Some of the possible print omission signs for which the general omission symbol should not be used in formal transcription, such as those in the problem, $\Box + \bigcirc = 5$, will be presented later, on page 69. Others can be found in the Code Book. If an omission sign is used for which the Code provides no representation, the transcriber may draw it in, or may devise a braille symbol to represent it. For classroom computation, however, the teacher may want to have the pupils use the general omission symbol whenever the print symbol has no specific mathematical significance, for the sake of speed and ease in reading and writing problems.

Practice Exercise

Transcribe the following problems, the last two in spatial arrangement:

Remember that a space must be left between an ellipsis or dash and a symbol of operation, as shown on page 31.

1. $3 + ? = 9$
2. $? - 0 = 5 - 4$
3. $3 \times 4 \ldots 12$
4. $-?- + -?- = 3$
5. "4 apples and 3 apples make ____."
6. $16 + \text{\underline{\ \ \ \ }} \times 2 = 36$

7. ____ is a short form of addition.
8. $2mn \cdot 3xy =$
9. $\begin{array}{r} 1692 \\ +\ ???? \\ \hline 7235 \end{array}$

10. $\dfrac{10}{4} = \dfrac{-?-}{-?-}$

Rule V – Type Forms

In the Nemeth Code, there are separate indicators for four special type forms: boldface, italic, sanserif, and script. Such variations in type form are transcribed only if the variant type has mathematical significance, assigning a different meaning to the letter or numeral or combination than it would have in regular type. The teacher will rarely be using them in transcribing materials for classroom use, and the blind student below college level will not often encounter them even in press-printed braille. The student using this manual is therefore referred simply to pages 36-41 of the Code Book for the appropriate rule in cases when he must read or transcribe variations in type form other than italic type in literary context, which follows the rules of literary braille.

Rule IV – Alphabets and Alphabetic Indicators

The Nemeth Code makes provision for five alphabets – English, German, Greek, Hebrew, and Russian. The English alphabet, and a few letters of the Greek alphabet which are used before college mathematics, are all that will be considered in this manual.

§ 24 The Greek-Letter Indicator

The Greek-Letter Indicator is dots 4-6. The letter follows it immediately if lower case. If capitalized, the "capitalization indicator," which is the capital sign of English Braille, is placed between the alphabetic indicator and the letter. In a sequence of Greek letters, an indicator is needed before each one.

⠨⠏ π, lower-case pi ⠨⠠⠎ Σ capitalized sigma

⠉⠕⠎⠀⠼⠆⠨⠹ cos 2θ – cos 2 theta, lower case

⠨⠑⠨⠙⠀⠙⠑⠋⠔⠊⠰⠝⠀⠷⠀⠇⠊⠍⠊⠞⠎

$\epsilon\delta$ definition of limits – epsilon delta, lower case

Copy the examples above.

§ 25 English Letter Indicator

The English-Letter Indicator is the same as the familiar "letter sign" of English Braille, and is used similarly, to distinguish single letters from their whole-word contractions, and certain combinations of letters from short-form words. It will be indicated hereafter by the abbreviation ELI.

§ 26 Use of the ELI

The ELI must be used with "single letters" or "short-form combinations." In the Code, a "single letter" is defined as:

i. an English letter in regular type,
ii. without any prime, subscript or superscript, or other modifier,
iii. and preceded and followed by a space or a mark of punctuation.

Letters written singly are not "single letters" unless they meet these specifications. A single-letter abbreviation or any of the single-letter words, *a, A, I,* or *O,* is not included in this definition.

A combination of letters such as *ab,* or *cd,* which might be mistaken for a short-form word, is called in the Code a "short-form letter combination," or more briefly, a "short-form combination," providing it is in lower case, in regular type, has no modifiers, and is preceded and followed by a space or a punctuation mark.

⠠⠑⠭⠻⠉⠊⠎⠑⠀⠼⠂⠤⠰⠁ Exercise 1-a

⠠⠮⠀⠎⠥⠍⠀⠷⠀⠰⠍⠀⠏⠇⠥⠎⠀⠰⠝ The sum of m plus n

⠰⠠⠭⠤⠠⠀⠰⠠⠽⠤⠠⠀⠯⠀⠰⠠⠵⠤⠁⠭⠑⠎⠲ X-, Y-, and Z-axes.

Note that a "single letter" is punctuated as a mathematical symbol, so that the mathematical comma follows it in the last example.

Rule IV – Alphabets and Alphabetic Indicators

⠀⠀⠀⠀⠀⠀⠀⠀⠀⠀⠀⠀⠀⠀⠀⠀⠀⠀⠀⠀⠀⠀⠀⠀⠀⠀⠀⠀⠀⠀⠀⠀⠀⠀⠀⠀ The intersection of ab and cd is R.

but:

⠀⠀⠀⠀⠀⠀⠀⠀⠀⠀⠀⠀⠀⠀⠀⠀⠀⠀⠀⠀⠀⠀⠀⠀⠀⠀⠀⠀⠀⠀⠀⠀⠀⠀⠀⠀⠀⠀⠀
The intersection of mn and pq is T.

Why are no ELI's required before the *mn* or the *pq*?

The PI must be used between the *R* and *T* and their periods in the last two examples because "single letters" are punctuated as mathematical symbols.

Copy the examples above and the last three on the previous page.

Application of the rules results in different use of the ELI in fractions arranged spatially and fractions in linear form. Look at the two sets below and analyze the reasons for use and non-use of the ELI in each.

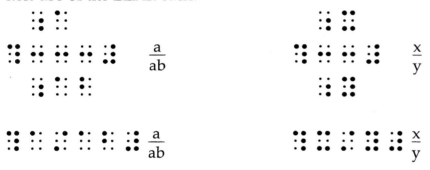

Copy the examples above.

§ 27 Non-Use of the ELI
This indicator is not used with a "single letter" or a "short-form combination" in these circumstances:
1. After a function name or its abbreviation

⠀⠀⠀⠀⠀⠀ cos A ⠀⠀⠀⠀⠀⠀⠀ log x

2. With the letter "s" when the *s* is part of the apostrophe-s combination.

⠀⠀⠀⠀⠀⠀⠀⠀⠀⠀⠀⠀⠀⠀⠀⠀⠀⠀⠀⠀⠀⠀⠀⠀ x's, y's, and z's.

38   Rule IV – Alphabets and Alphabetic Indicators

3. If the "single letter" or "short-form combination" is preceded or followed by a comparison symbol.

If a = b, then ac = bc.

a, b, and c = 10

e × e = e-squared

4. With any letter or combination of letters which are neither "single letters" nor "short-form combinations" in situations not specifically covered in Rule IV, § 26 and 27. (Not all situations given in the Code Book have been covered here. Additional rules will be given later, in connection with additional symbols and their uses.)

Copy all the examples in § 27.

§ 28,b Use of the ELI with Letters Having Special Endings
When only one letter or any combination of unspaced letters has a plural, possessive, or ordinal ending, the ELI must be used or not used as if those endings were not present. It is not used immediately before such endings. Explain its use in the examples below.

xs   x's   nth   6nth

Copy these examples.

§ 28,c The ELI with Roman Numerals
In Nemeth Code, capitalized Roman numerals of more than one letter are written as in English Braille, preceded by double capital dots without the ELI. Lower-case Roman numerals are treated as one letter even when they consist of more than one, and are governed by the rules for use of the ELI with any letter. This is also true for single capitalized Roman numerals. Justify the use or non-use of the ELI in each example below.

Ex. iv   III + V

i, ii, iii

but:

I, II, III.

Copy these examples.

Rule IV – Alphabets and Alphabetic Indicators

§ 29 Letters in Diagrams
When a single English letter in regular type is used as a label in a diagram or drawing, the ELI is required if the letter is in lower case, but not if the letter is capitalized.

§ 30 Letters in Tables
When letters appear in tables, whether as entries or headings, follow the regular rules to determine use or non-use of the ELI.

Summary of Rules on Use of the ELI
Use the ELI:

    i. with "single letters" and "short-form combinations" unless they are preceded or followed by a sign of comparison;

    ii. with all lower-case Roman numerals, and with an upper-case Roman numeral consisting of only one letter, in accordance with the rules for any letter;

    iii. with single lower-case letters in diagrams.

Do NOT use the ELI:

    i. with "single letters" or "short-form combinations" that are preceded or followed by a sign of comparison;

    ii. with "single letters" or "short-form combinations" that follow a function name or abbreviation;

    iii. before the *s* of an apostrophe-s combination;

    iv. before plural, possessive or ordinal endings that follow one letter or a group of unspaced letters;

    v. with single upper-case letters in diagrams.

Practice Exercise
Transcribe these problems. Use linear format for all fractions except the last. (Find the Greek letter "mu" on page 24 of the Code Book.)

1. If an arc has measure q and radius r, then its length is $L = \dfrac{q}{180} \cdot r$.

2. The years L-LX.

3. $\dfrac{x}{y}$

4. the mnth part

5. Page vii

6. Find the value of x.

7. $\dfrac{ab}{b} = a$

8. X's, Y's, Z's.

9. $cd = c \cdot d$

10. tan x

11. μ, the Greek letter "mu," stands for "micron." $1\ \mu = \dfrac{1}{1,000,000}$.

12. $\dfrac{x}{xy}$

Rule III – Capitalization

§ 20-22 Use of the Capitalization Indicator

Two points need to be made regarding use of the "Capitalization Indicator" of the Nemeth Code. In most respects its use corresponds with the use of the capital sign of English Braille.

1. Capitalization must not be used with a letter just because it begins a sentence, if it is not capitalized in print.

⠭ ⠊⠎ ⠁ ⠝⠥⠍⠃⠻ ⠃⠑⠞⠺⠑⠢ ⠼⠃ ⠯ ⠼⠉⠲

x is a number between 2 and 3.

2. A single capitalization indicator applies only to the letter which follows it, so one is needed before each individual letter in a capitalized sequence, except with Roman numerals and abbreviations. These are capitalized in the same manner as in English Braille.

⠫ ⠠⠁⠠⠃⠠⠉   angle ABC   ⠠⠠⠊⠊⠊   III

⠠⠎⠠⠁⠠⠎   SAS – (side-angle-side)

Remember that a PI is required between a mark of punctuation and a sequence in which each letter has a separate identity.

Copy the examples above.

Practice Exercise

Transcribe the following problems:

1. MDCCC + L

2. 8:40 MST – Mountain Standard Time

3. HL, Hypotenuse-leg

4. Are the diagonals equal in the parallelogram QRST?

Rule VIII – Abbreviations

Most abbreviations are written in Nemeth Code the same as in English Braille, using literary punctuation, with no PI before the period.

Mon., Feb. 9, 2 p.m.
Notice the use of a literary comma after the abbreviation, a math comma after the numeral.

Ph.D. e.g.

G. B. Shaw

Washington, D.C.

lcd – least common denominator

L.U.B. – Least Upper Bound

ClPA – Closure Property for Addition

d-c – direct current

RCA

§ 49, ii Abbreviations of Measurement
In Nemeth Code, abbreviations of measurement are written as in print in most cases. They do not precede the Numeric Indicator, as in English Braille, and an *s*, if present in print, is included in the transcription.

25 sq. ft. 100 lbs.

Copy the examples in the sections above.

§ 51 ELI with Abbreviations
When an abbreviation consists of one letter or a combination of letters corresponding to a short-form word, and is followed by a period which applies to the abbreviation, no ELI is necessary before it. Sometimes a period follows an abbreviation but only marks the end of the sentence and does not apply to the abbreviation itself, as in the fourth example on page 42. In this case, and wherever an abbreviation of one letter or of letters corresponding to a short-form word is not followed by a period which applies to it, the ELI must be used. If it is not clear whether the period applies to the abbreviation, assume that it does and transcribe accordingly.

Does 1 km. = 1000 m.?

(braille)   1 km = 1000 m

(braille)   1 light-yr

(braille) $\dfrac{m}{cm} \times \dfrac{cm}{mm}$

(braille)

(braille)   32 degrees F = 0 degrees C.

How can you tell that the period ends the sentence and does not apply to the abbreviation?

(braille)   12 mo. = 1 yr.

(braille) $\dfrac{w.}{v.}$ weight divided by volume

§ 54 Spacing with Abbreviations

As illustrated in the foregoing examples, a space must be left on either side of an abbreviation except for punctuation and any indicator, fraction line, slash line or grouping symbol which applies to it. Even symbols of operation other than the fraction line or the slash must be spaced from abbreviations. The slash and various grouping symbols will be presented later on in this manual.

(braille)   10 g + 10 g = 20 g

No space is left between components of an abbreviation when no space appears in print, as already shown in *p.m., cm, km.* etc.

Remember that a numeral following a hyphen that follows an abbreviation must be preceded by the NI. See page 32, § 9, f.

(braille) $5\frac{1}{2}$ ft.-2 yds.

Abbreviations of reference are not condensed in Nemeth Braille as they are in English Braille.

(braille)

See Chap. IV, p. 27.

(braille)

Find Vol. I, pp. 30-35.

Copy the examples on this page.

Rule VIII – Abbreviations

§ 53 Contractions in Abbreviations
See pages 52-53.

§ 49, b Non-Abbreviations
A letter or sequence of letters that does not represent a word or phrase is not an abbreviation and must be transcribed according to other rules of the Code. This applies also to abbreviated function names, model numbers, serial numbers, etc.

⠠⠃⠥⠽ ⠎⠕⠍⠑ ⠠⠧⠊⠞⠁⠍⠊⠝ ⠠⠁⠲ Buy some Vitamin A.

⠠⠃⠇⠕⠕⠙ ⠞⠽⠏⠑⠎ ⠁⠗⠑ ⠠⠁⠂ ⠠⠃⠂ ⠠⠁⠠⠃⠂ ⠁⠝⠙ ⠠⠕⠲ Blood types are A, B, AB, and O.

⠉⠕⠎ ⠭ cos x

⠠⠎⠻⠊⠁⠇ ⠝⠕⠲ ⠠⠛⠑⠼⠊⠋⠼⠃ Serial no. GE96F12

As in an example on page 15, the Multipurpose Indicator, dot 5, is used between *E* and *96* and between *F* and *12* to prevent the numerals from being read as subscripts. See pages 72 and 85.

Copy the examples above.

Practice Exercise
Transcribe the problems below.

1. LASER, Light Amplification by Stimulated Emission of Radiation.

2. Dr. John M. Crandell

3. $1\frac{7}{8}$ i.p.s.

4. 1 g = 32 ft per sec, per sec

5. 3 ft. = -?- yds.

6. Refer to footnote 23, Vol. II, Sec. X, p. 196.

7. $\tan = \dfrac{\text{opp.}}{\text{adj.}}$

8. GCF, Greatest Common Factor

9. How many points must the team score to win the class B cup?

10. 14 oz. + 2 oz. = 1 lb.

Rule XVIII – Signs and Symbols of Grouping

The print signs of grouping most often encountered in school mathematics, and their Nemeth counterparts, are shown below. The Nemeth symbols must be used throughout mathematical transcriptions, even in literary context. The grouping symbols of English Braille (parentheses and square brackets) are used only to enclose literary material on title pages.

⠸⠣ ⠜ ⠣ ⠜ ⠣ ⠜ ⠸⠜   Parentheses (round brackets) (   )

⠈⠣ ⠸⠣ ⠣ ⠜ ⠣ ⠜ ⠸⠜   Brackets (square brackets) [   ]

⠨⠣ ⠸⠣ ⠣ ⠜ ⠣ ⠜ ⠸⠜   Braces (curly brackets) {   }

⠶⠶ ⠶⠶   (i.e.)   ⠈⠣⠴⠠⠀⠂�000�402��   [0, 1]

⠸⠣⠠⠺⠑⠙⠲⠠⠀⠠⠞⠓⠥⠗⠎⠲⠠⠀⠠⠋⠗⠊⠲⠸⠜   {Wed., Thurs., Fri.}

Rule II, § 10 The Enclosed List

The use or non-use of the NI and ELI with items enclosed in grouping symbols depends on whether or not the grouping is an "enclosed list" as defined in Nemeth Code. It is therefore essential to learn the specifications for an "enclosed list" in order to write or transcribe correctly the expressions within any grouping symbols.

An "enclosed list" consists of:
- i. two or more items within grouping symbols,
- ii. the items separated by commas,
- iii. the items including no word, ordinal ending, plural ending, sign of comparison, or abbreviation (except an abbreviated function name), and
- iv. the items including no mark of punctuation other than the commas.

If a grouping does not meet all these requirements, it is not an "enclosed list."

Rule II, § 11 The NI with Items Enclosed in Grouping Symbols

The NI is not used at the beginning of an item in an "enclosed list." If the grouping is not an "enclosed list," the NI is used according to the other rules of the code.

Decide which groupings below are "enclosed lists." Be able to tell why.

⠈⠣⠢⠑⠤⠔⠡⠌⠎⠞⠊⠩��⠜   [5-inch stick]

⠷⠤⠂⠠⠀⠤⠆⠠⠀⠤⠒⠾   (−1, −2, −3)

⠨⠣⠴⠠⠀⠤⠂⠠⠀⠬⠆⠨⠜   {0, −1, + 2}

⠷⠂⠀⠆⠀⠒⠾   (1   2   3)

⠷⠂⠬⠓⠠⠀⠆⠬�6⠠⠀⠴⠾   (1 + h, 2 + k, 0)

⠂⠀⠽⠙⠲⠀⠷⠒⠀⠋⠞⠲⠾   1 yd. (3 ft.)

Copy all examples on this page.

Rule XVIII – Signs and Symbols of Grouping

Rule IV, § 27, d The ELI with Items Enclosed in Grouping Symbols

The ELI must not be used with a "single letter" or "short-form combination" which is an item in an "enclosed list."

(0, a, 1, b, 2)

{a, b, c, d}

[ab, cd]

(a, 2x, b)

(a = 1, b = 2, c = − 4)

Is this an enclosed list? Explain.

Rule II, § 10 Signs of Omission in an Enclosed List

An item in an "enclosed list" may be indicated by the ellipsis or any other symbol used for omission.

{a, b, ... , j}

(x + 1, x + 2, ?, ?, x + 5)

(4, 8, 12,   )

A function name such as *sine, cosine, tangent, logarithm,* or an abbreviated function name *(sin, cos, tan, log)* and the signs that follow it, are considered a single item in an "enclosed list."

(log x, log y)

An "enclosed list" of two items.

When some of the items in a long "enclosed list" must run over to a second line, the NI is not needed before the first item on the new line.

(1, 2, 3, 4, 5, 6, 7, 8, 9, 10, 11, 12)

Copy the examples on this page.

Rule XVIII – Signs and Symbols of Grouping

Rule IV § 28, a The ELI and Groupings Other Than "Enclosed Lists"

The ELI must not be used when only one letter or any combination of unspaced letters is in direct contact with both its opening and closing grouping signs. This includes letters expressing Roman numerals.

⠿ ⠿ ⠿ ⠿   1.

     ⠿ ⠿ ⠿   (a)

     ⠿ ⠿ ⠿   (b)

⠿ ⠿ ⠿ ⠿ ⠿ ⠿ ⠿ ⠿ ⠿   (ab) + (cd)

⠿ ⠿ ⠿ ⠿ ⠿ ⠿ ⠿   [iii]

⠿ ⠿ ⠿ ⠿ ⠿ ⠿   (XL)

⠿ ⠿ ⠿ ⠿   (V)

A choice between the singular and plural form of a word is sometimes shown by enclosing an *s* within parentheses after it.

⠿ ⠿ ⠿ ⠿ ⠿ ⠿ ⠿ ⠿ ⠿ ⠿ ⠿ ⠿ ⠿ ⠿ ⠿ ⠿ ⠿ ⠿ ⠿

Which principle(s) applies here?

When only one letter or any combination of unspaced letters is in direct contact with only the opening or only the closing grouping sign, the ELI is used or not used as though the grouping sign were not present.

⠿ ⠿ ⠿ ⠿ ⠿ ⠿ ⠿ ⠿ ⠿ ⠿   (ab = cd) (Why are no ELIs used?)

⠿ ⠿

(p is a positive integer)

⠿ ⠿ ⠿ ⠿ ⠿ ⠿ ⠿ ⠿ ⠿ ⠿ ⠿ ⠿ ⠿   [x-intercept]

⠿ ⠿ ⠿ ⠿ ⠿ ⠿ ⠿ ⠿   (iv - v)

⠿ ⠿ ⠿ ⠿ ⠿ ⠿ ⠿ ⠿ ⠿   (mn; xy)

Copy the examples on this page.

Rule XVIII – Signs and Symbols of Grouping 47

Review of Signs and Symbols of Grouping

1. Material within grouping symbols constitutes an "enclosed list" if it:
   i. includes at least two items, separated by commas, and
   ii. contains no other punctuation, no comparison sign, and no word, abbreviation, ordinal or plural ending.

2. In an "enclosed list":
   i. Do not use the NI at the beginning of a numeric item;
   ii. Do not use the ELI before a "single letter" or a "short-form combination."

3. If the grouping is not an enclosed list:
   i. Use the NI according to other rules of the Code;
   ii. Do not use the ELI with one letter or more unspaced letters in direct contact with both the opening and closing grouping signs;
   iii. Ignore the grouping sign and follow general rules on use of the ELI if one letter or more unspaced letters is in direct contact with only the opening or only the closing grouping sign.

4. Any symbol used for omission may be an item in an "enclosed list."

5. A function name or its abbreviation, plus the signs associated with it, counts as a single item in an "enclosed list."

6. In a runover of an "enclosed list" of numerals, do not use the NI at the beginning of the new line.

Practice Exercise

Transcribe the following problems involving the use of grouping symbols. In each case, state whether or not the grouping is an "enclosed list." If you decide it is not, tell why, and give the rule you are following in using or not using the ELI or the NI.

1. $(4\frac{1}{2}, 5, x)$
2. $(a = 1, b = 2)$
3. Rule V, Sec. 8, (a)
4. $[n(4 + 3)(7 + 3)]$
5. $(u, v; x, y)$
6. (1st, 2nd, 3rd)
7. $(\cos m, \cos n, \cos p)$
8. $(6 + 2, 2 + 2)$
9. $\{1, 3, 5, \ldots, 15\}$
10. (a, ab, b, c, cd)
11. $[-1, 1; -2, 2]$
12. $(a\text{-}z)$
13. $(x, \quad , z)$
14. $(x$ is the unknown quantity.$)$
15. Metric weights (g., cg., mg.)
16. $A = \{circle, rectangle, triangle\}$
17. (3's, 6's, 9's)
18. Underline any prime number(s) in the group.

§ 124 Vertical Bars As Grouping Symbols

Single vertical bars are often read as *the absolute value of.* They also have other uses. Double vertical bars, sometimes in boldface type, are usually read as *the norm of* (in connection with *vectors* in high school mathematics).

⠿ ⠀ ⠀ ⠀ ⠿   single vertical bars| |

⠿ ⠿ ⠀ ⠀ ⠀ ⠿ ⠿   double vertical bars‖ ‖ (See p. 126, Code Book, for boldface version.)

⠿ ⠀ ⠿ |x| (the absolute value of x)

⠿ ⠿ ⠀ ⠿ ⠿   ‖f‖ (the norm of f)

§ 125 Transcriber's Grouping Symbols

Whenever the transcriber inserts an explanatory note into text material, the note must be enclosed within transcriber's grouping symbols, dot 6 in one cell followed by dot 3 in the next. The material within these symbols follows the same rules as within other grouping symbols. If a note consists of seven words or less it may be inserted into the text at the point where it applies. Longer notes must be placed at the nearest convenient point and must be placed, indented, and run over in accordance with the rules of the *Code of Braille Textbook Formats and Techniques.*

⠀ ⠿ ⠀ ⠿ ⠀ ⠿ ⠀ ⠀ ⠿ ⠿ ⠿ ⠿ ⠀ ⠀ ⠀ ⠀ ⠀ ⠀ ⠿ ⠿ ⠿ ⠀ ⠿   Count the fathers.

⠿ ⠀ ⠿ ⠀ ⠿ ⠀ ⠀ ⠀ ⠿ ⠿ ⠀ ⠀ ⠀ ⠀ ⠿ ⠿ ⠿ ⠀ ⠀   Shown as dot 5, f, below.

The last sentence represents a note inserted by the transcriber.

§ 126 Enlarged Grouping Symbols

Enlarged grouping signs used in print to unify systems of equations, determinants, and matrices arranged on two or more lines of print may be indicated in braille by adding dot 6 to the grouping symbol, or by drawing in the enlarged grouping sign. See p. 126, Code Book.

Rule XVIII – Signs and Symbols of Grouping

Rule VI, § 37, xiv Punctuation and Grouping Symbols

A comma which follows a grouping symbol is a mathematical comma. Other marks of punctuation, except the hyphen, dash and ellipsis, must be preceded by the PI.

Study paragraphs (1), (2), and (6).

What is the least common denominator (LCD)?

Copy the examples above.

Practice Exercise
Transcribe these problems:

1. Is this (a), (b), or (c)?

2. $|-10|$

3. Which arrangement of chairs in the diagram below will seat the most students?
   Transcriber's note: The symbol "of" represents one chair.

Rule IX – Contractions and Short-Form Words

§ 56 Use of Contractions and Short-Form Words
As you have observed in many examples already shown, the contractions of English Braille are usually employed in the Nemeth Code, according to the standard rules.

§ 55, a Non-Use of Contractions and Short-Form Words
In general, contractions or short-form words are not used in a word, part of a word, or abbreviation that precedes or follows a Nemeth symbol without a space between. The rule applies even when transition to a new line separates the two items in question. Specifically, this restriction includes:

1. Any braille indicator other than capitalization indicators or the italic sign of English Braille.

$$\frac{distance}{time} = rate$$

Note that in spatial arrangements, the words of fractions are not in contact with the fraction indicators, and contractions may be used.

$$rate = \frac{distance}{time}$$

2. The general omission symbol.

ten ? four = six

3. Any operation symbol.

nine – seven = two

population ÷ people who own cars

Copy the examples above.

Rule IX – Contractions and Short-Form Words

4. Any comparison symbol, even though a space intervenes between it and the word, part word, or abbreviation.

⠿⠀(braille)⠀⠀⠀1 hour = 60 minutes

(braille)

Let 3x = the larger number

(braille)⠀⠀⠀seven + three = ten

(braille)

(braille)

It is a fundamental principle that ='s added to ='s are =.

    Explain each non-use of a contraction in the example above. Note application of the restriction in spite of transition to a new line.

(braille)

(braille)

Total amount paid = sum of 5 checks received.

(braille)

(braille)

(braille)

$$\text{gas mileage on journey} = \frac{\text{distance traveled}}{\text{amount of gas used}}$$

Identify the different factors that limit contractions in this example.

5. Any modifier symbol. (See pages 75-76.)

6. The radical symbol. (See page 78.)

Note that Nemeth grouping symbols are not included in the above list of symbols which restrict the use of contractions. See pages 57-58 for a complete discussion of contractions in contact with grouping symbols.

Copy all examples on pages 50 and 51.

§ 55, b Contractions with Function Names

Contractions must not be used in abbreviated function names in any context, nor in unabbreviated function names in mathematical context. Remember to use the PI before punctuation that follows a function name in mathematical context or an abbreviated function name in any context.

⠠⠎⠊⠝⠀⠭ sin x

⠉⠕⠎⠓⠀⠭ cosh x

⠎⠊⠝⠑⠀⠭⠀⠲⠀⠎⠊⠝⠑⠀⠽ sine x + sine y

⠼⠃⠀⠁⠗⠉⠎⠊⠝⠀⠭ 2 arcsin x

⠠⠁⠗⠉⠀⠠⠎⠊⠝⠑⠀⠭ Arc Sine x

Arc ACB is a major arc.

Justify the two different transcriptions of *arc*. Why does no PI follow the second?

The abbreviation for "sine" is "sin."

Note that "sine" is contracted in literary context.

Copy the first two and the last two examples above.

§ 53 Contractions in Abbreviations

No contraction may be used in an abbreviation which is in *direct* contact with any of the items in § 55, a, but an intervening period which applies to the abbreviation makes the use of the contraction permissible. The rule applies when abbreviations precede or follow symbols of operation, even though there must be a space between them (page 42).

240 min ÷ 60

15 min. × 4 = ?

$$\frac{1 \text{ hr.}}{60 \text{ min.}}$$

but

$$\frac{1 \text{ hr}}{60 \text{ min}}$$

1 cent. + 10 yrs. = 11 decades

Copy these examples.

Rule IX – Contractions and Short-Form Words

The abbreviation *in.* or *in* for *inch* or *inches* must never be contracted. The *st* contraction may be used for abbreviating *street* or *saint,* but not for any other abbreviation.

27 in   12-in. ruler

Using the chart above, measure Main St.

1 st. (stone) = 14 lbs.

Contractions may not be used in acronyms.

FORTRAN   MASER

Copy all examples.

Review the rules restricting use of contractions presented and illustrated thus far by completing the summary below, omitting reference to the modifier and radical symbols, which you have not yet learned:

Contractions and short-form words are not used in words, part words or abbreviations just before or after:

1. braille indicators

2.

3.

4.

nor in:

1. abbreviated function names, or

2.

54   **Rule IX – Contractions and Short-Form Words**

Practice Exercise
Transcribe the problems below. After each, write briefly the rule you have applied in connection with contractions.

1. 1 sec. long. $= \dfrac{1}{15}$ sec. time

2. 5n means $5 \times n$.

3. 2sine x + 3cosine y

4. 365 days = 1 yr

5. 69 = 6 tens, 9 ones

6. 1 yr = 365 days

7. 24 in. ÷ 12 = 2 in.

8. distance ÷ time =

9. sin x + y

10. four -?- eight = twelve

12. LASER

11. n st. angles (*st.* for *straight*)

13. Parents plus children = total members in family.

14. horsepower $= \dfrac{\text{force} \times \text{distance}}{\text{time in seconds} \times 550}$ (Transcribe in linear and spatial arrangement.)

15. The square of the hypotenuse = the sum of the squares of the other two sides.

§ 55, c. *To, into,* and *by* in Nemeth Code
These contractions are limited as in the rules above, and in addition must not be used before:

1. Any word, part word, or abbreviation in which contractions may not be used.

⠿ ⠿ ⠿ ⠿ ⠿   ⠿ ⠿ ⠿ ⠿ ⠿ ⠿ ⠿ ⠿ ⠿   ⠿ ⠿   ⠿ ⠿ ⠿ ⠿

people coming by car + people coming by bus

(The *ar* sign is not used in *car* because the word is in contact with the plus sign. *By* may therefore not be contracted before it.)

⠿ ⠿ ⠿ ⠿ ⠿ ⠿ ⠿ ⠿ ⠿ ⠿ ⠿ ⠿ ⠿ ⠿ ⠿ ⠿ ⠿ ⠿ ⠿   miles to town = ?

2. Any abbreviation which consists of only one letter or of a short-form combination.

⠿ ⠿

⠿ ⠿ ⠿ ⠿ ⠿ ⠿ ⠿ ⠿ ⠿ ⠿   Write the formula for converting F. to C.

⠿ ⠿ ⠿ ⠿ ⠿ ⠿ ⠿ ⠿ ⠿ ⠿ ⠿ ⠿ ⠿ ⠿ ⠿ ⠿ ⠿ ⠿   Convert days into yrs.

Note the contraction of the *in* in *into*.

Rule IX – Contractions and Short-Form Words

3. A Roman numeral.

⠀⠀⠀⠀⠀⠀⠀⠀⠀⠀⠀⠀⠀⠀⠀⠀⠀⠀⠀⠀⠀⠀⠀⠀⠀⠀⠀⠀   Chapters I to VII.

4. A numeric symbol written as in Nemeth Code.

⠀⠀⠀⠀⠀⠀⠀⠀⠀⠀⠀⠀⠀⠀⠀⠀⠀⠀⠀⠀⠀⠀⠀⠀⠀   Divide 49 by 7.

⠀⠀⠀⠀⠀⠀⠀⠀⠀⠀⠀⠀⠀⠀⠀⠀⠀⠀   Add 16 to 25.

5. A dash or ellipsis.

⠀⠀⠀⠀⠀⠀⠀⠀⠀⠀⠀⠀⠀⠀⠀⠀⠀⠀⠀⠀⠀⠀⠀⠀⠀⠀⠀⠀⠀

20 added to ____ equals 30

6. A "single letter."

⠀⠀⠀⠀⠀⠀⠀⠀⠀⠀⠀⠀⠀⠀⠀⠀⠀⠀⠀⠀⠀⠀⠀⠀⠀⠀⠀⠀⠀⠀⠀⠀⠀⠀⠀

The imaginary part denoted by i = ?

Why is there no ELI before *i*?

7. A sequence of mathematical letters in which each has a separate identity.

⠀⠀⠀⠀⠀⠀⠀⠀⠀⠀⠀⠀⠀⠀⠀⠀⠀⠀⠀⠀⠀⠀⠀⠀⠀⠀   BC is parallel to DE

8. Any abbreviated function name, or unabbreviated function name in mathematical context.

⠀⠀⠀⠀⠀⠀⠀⠀⠀⠀⠀⠀⠀⠀⠀⠀⠀⠀⠀⠀⠀⠀⠀⠀⠀⠀⠀⠀⠀⠀⠀

y is proportional to log x.

9. Any grouping symbol.

⠀⠀⠀⠀⠀⠀⠀⠀⠀⠀⠀⠀   from (1) to (5)

Copy the examples above.

56   **Rule IX – Contractions and Short-Form Words**

    Review the rules just presented governing use of the contractions for *to, into,* and *by.* Complete this summary:

These words may not be contracted before mathematical expressions in general, and specifically before:

1.   6.

2.   7.

3.   8.

4.   9.

5.

Practice Exercise
Transcribe these problems involving *to, into,* and *by.* State the rule applied.

  1. Convert ft. to in.   2. 144 divided by ... = 12

  3. The sum is denoted by S.

                                   4. $\dfrac{\text{total distance}}{\text{distance to store}}$

  5. VII to X

                              6. {5, 10, 15} intersected by {4, 6, 8} = $\underline{?}$

  7. Change oz. to g.

                              8. What is the relationship of cos x to sin x?

  9. Extend ray AB to C.

                           10. Divide your paper into 2-in. squares.

11. Multiply by 12.

                         12. $\frac{1}{2}$ hr. converted into min.

13. 1-to-1 correspondence

                         14. Is ABC congruent to XYZ?

15. Carry your answer to 3 decimal places.

§ 55, d Contractions in Ordinal Endings
The *st* and *th* contractions must not be used for ordinal endings attached to numerals, letters, or other mathematical expressions. If an ordinal ending is composed of only one letter in print, write it the same way in braille.

⠿   1st, 2nd, 3rd, 4th.

⠿ ⠿ ⠿ ⠿ ⠿   2nth   ⠿ ⠿ ⠿ ⠿ ⠿ ⠿ ⠿ ⠿ ⠿ ⠿ ⠿ ⠿   1st and 2d.

Copy the examples above.

Rule IX – Contractions and Short-Form Words

§ 55, e Contractions in Contact with Grouping Symbols

1. The whole-word alphabet contractions for *but, can, do, . . . , you, as,* and the whole-word lower sign contractions for *be, enough, his, in, was, were, to, into* and *by* must not be used in direct contact with any grouping symbol. *Enough, were* and *into* may be partially contracted.

A = {every prime number from 1 to 50}

(people who do not know French) - (people who do)

(in factoring)

(it may never be)

Divide evenly (into four parts).

2. The contractions for *and, for, of, the, with,* whether used as whole words or part words, must not be used in direct contact with any grouping symbol, and when they may not be used as part words because of this rule, no other contractions may be used in the words affected.

(the additive inverse)

(with the third group)

[theorem 5]

(force of gravity)

(often used to denote "absolute value")

These contractions may be used in a word which is in contact with a grouping symbol if the contraction itself is not in contact with the grouping symbol.

(officially withdrawn)

Compare the *of* and the *with*.

Copy all the examples on this page.

Rule IX – Contractions and Short-Form Words

3. An intervening capital, italic sign, or mark of punctuation does not affect the rules of § 55, e, just given.

(Will 7 be an element of this set?)

(*Be sure* to add the sales tax.)

(How many more?)

Copy these three examples.

4. Contractions *are* used in words or abbreviations in contact with math grouping symbols unless other limiting factors presented in § 55 are involved. They are also used in a literary word joined to a mathematical term by a hyphen.

(rate) × (time) = (distance)

(ft.-pound)

$\frac{1}{2}$-off sale

9-inch

{red, green, yellow}

§ 55, f Contractions Resembling Mathematical Expressions
Contractions must not be used when they could be mistaken for mathematical expressions.

Can C = 100?

n = − 2, not + 2

Copy the examples above.

Rule IX – Contractions and Short-Form Words

Practice Exercise

Transcribe these problems, using italics where indicated. Be able to justify use and non-use of contractions.

1. time *(in seconds)*

2. She bought a 2-yard remnant.

3. {twenty, thirty, forty}

4. (What remainder will you have?)

5. Prove that t = 0.

6. [(Art, Ed) (Ben, Will)]

7. even numbers (from 2 to 20)

8. Sold for fifty dollars *(the best offer).*

9. (force × distance)

10. the small box (pound size)

11. (as illustrated below)

12. (It is specified that q is a positive number.)

13. $\dfrac{\text{(cost of all)}}{\text{(cost of one)}} = $ (number bought)

14. (a reasonable estimate of what the quotient will be)

15. rod (a measure of land)

16. (third theorem)

Rule XX – Signs and Symbols of Comparison

You already know the equals sign. Other comparison signs frequently used in school mathematics, and their braille symbols, are given below. Remember that a symbol of comparison must be preceded and followed by a space, unless an indicator or a symbol of grouping or punctuation applies to it, and that contractions may not be used in words or abbreviations that precede or follow symbols of comparison. Notice the similarity of many of the braille shapes to their print equivalents.

§ 139 Negation

A negation sign is frequently used in conjunction with a comparison sign, represented in print by a vertical stroke or by an oblique stroke in either direction. However the negation is represented in print, it is always transcribed in braille by dots 3, 4, unspaced before the comparison symbol affected.

Is not equal to ($\neq$)　⠿⠿⠿　⠿⠿⠿⠿⠿⠿⠿⠿⠿⠿⠿⠿　$C \neq B.$

Is less than ($<$)　⠿⠿　⠿⠿⠿⠿⠿⠿　$x < y$

Is not less than ($\not<$)　⠿⠿⠿　⠿⠿⠿⠿⠿⠿⠿⠿　$x \not< 4$

Is less than or equal to ($\leqq$)　⠿⠿⠿⠿

⠿⠿⠿⠿⠿⠿⠿⠿⠿⠿⠿⠿　$(a + b) \leqq 9$

Is greater than ($>$)　⠿⠿　Is not greater than ($\not>$)　⠿⠿⠿

Is greater than or equal to ($\geqq$)　⠿⠿⠿⠿

Is approximately equal to (double tilde) ($\approx$)　⠿⠿⠿⠿

⠿⠿⠿⠿⠿⠿⠿⠿⠿⠿⠿⠿⠿⠿⠿⠿⠿⠿⠿⠿⠿⠿

$1 \text{ mm} \approx \dfrac{1}{25} \text{ in}$ (One millimeter is approximately equal to one twenty-fifth of an inch.)

Identity (is congruent to; is identically equal to) ($\equiv$)　⠿⠿

⠿⠿⠿⠿⠿⠿⠿⠿⠿⠿⠿⠿　$f(x) \equiv 0$

Congruence ("is related to") ($\cong$) (Implies some variance)　⠿⠿⠿⠿

⠿⠿⠿⠿⠿⠿⠿⠿⠿⠿⠿⠿⠿⠿⠿⠿⠿⠿⠿⠿⠿⠿⠿⠿⠿⠿⠿⠿

angle ABC $\cong$ angle DEF

Ratio ("is to") (:)　⠿⠿　Proportion ("as") (::)　⠿⠿

⠿⠿⠿⠿⠿⠿⠿⠿⠿⠿⠿⠿⠿⠿⠿⠿⠿⠿⠿⠿⠿⠿　$1 : 2 :: 3 : 6$

Rule XX – Signs and Symbols of Comparison. 61

Inclusion, Reverse Inclusion, Membership, and Vertical Bar *(such that):* see under Set Notation, page 65.

For other comparison signs, see Code Book, pages 134-44.

The PI must be used before a mark of punctuation that follows a sign of comparison. This combination seldom occurs, however.

The symbol for "is less than" is "<."

Practice Exercise
Transcribe the following:

1. a = b, but b ≠ c

2. ay ≅ az

3. y ⊀ (6 × 2)

4. $\frac{8}{3} > \frac{5}{3}$

5. a < b < c means that the point b is between point a and point c on the number line.

6. m : n :: 5 : ?

7. [(3 + 4)(5 + 2)] < (m + n)

8. 2 ≡ 5(mod 3)

9. Is 1 km > or < 1 mi?

10. 1 liter ≈ 1 quart

11. If m > 0, then |m| = m.

Rule XXII – Miscellaneous Signs and Symbols

Cents (¢)　⠀⠀⠀⠀　　10¢

Note difference in position from that in literary braille.

Dollars ($)　⠀⠀⠀⠀　　$2.98

For spatial arrangement of problems that include dollar signs, see the Code Book, § 178, b, page 162, and examples on page 164.

At (@)　⠀⠀⠀⠀　　3 boxes @ 27¢

Note that a space is left on each side.

Precent (%)　⠀⠀⠀⠀　　7%

Also positioned differently from literary braille.

Prime (′)　⠀⠀⠀⠀　　x'

The single and double primes are also used to express feet and inches, and minutes and seconds of time or of angle.

⠀⠀⠀⠀⠀⠀　　5′8″ (5 feet, 8 inches, or 5 minutes, 8 seconds)

Note that there is no space between prime symbols nor between a prime and the quantity to which it applies.

Degree (°) The small elevated circle used as the sign for degrees, as in 70°, is a superscript. The braille symbol for it is given in the section on Rule XIII, p. 74 of this manual.

Since (∵)　⠀⠀⠀　　Therefore (∴)　⠀⠀⠀

Therefore, negated ("It does not follow that")(/∴)　⠀⠀⠀
Note similarity to print shapes.

⠀⠀⠀⠀⠀⠀⠀⠀⠀⠀⠀⠀⠀⠀⠀⠀⠀⠀⠀⠀⠀⠀

∵ a = b and b = c ∴ a = c

Copy the examples above.

Rule XXII – Miscellaneous Signs and Symbols

Tally Marks (|) ⠒⠂

Tally marks are grouped as in print, with an additional tally replacing the cross tally often used for the fifth tally in print. Groups are separated from each other by one space, and also from surrounding material except applicable punctuation, indicators, and grouping symbols.

Transition to a new line must not be made within a group of tallies.

The Multipurpose Indicator, dot 5, must be used between a tally mark and the PI.

Ditto Mark (″) ⠂ ⠒

A space is left on each side of the ditto mark. The symbol is centered under the word or numerals, etc. to be duplicated. This may necessitate altering the normal spacing in the line above the ditto marks.

2 goes into 2, 1

″   ″   ″ 4, 2

″   ″   ″ 6, 3

The contractions for *to, into,* and *by* may not be used before any of the miscellaneous symbols of Rule XXII.

The PI must be used before punctuation that follows any of these miscellaneous symbols.

Convert this fraction to %.

Copy the examples above.

64   Rule XXII – Miscellaneous Signs and Symbols

The crosshatch and slash are not under Miscellaneous Symbols in the Code, but are included here as additional convenient symbols:

Number Sign (crosshatch) (#) ("pounds" [weight])

⠨⠼   #6 (number 6)   4# (lbs.)

The need to repeat the NI makes the braille form less useful than the number sign in print.

Slash or Diagonal Line ("per") (/)

    How many mi./hr.?

This symbol is also the diagonal fraction line.

The slash is a symbol of operation, and requires no space on either side of it. In Nemeth Code context, the Nemeth symbol must be used, never the literary one.

    and/or (not as in literary braille)

    c/o ("care of")

    10/23/79 (a date)

Copy the examples on this page.

Practice Exercise
Transcribe these problems:
1. 15¢ is ?% of $1.20?

2. Light travels at the rate of 186,000 mi/sec.

3. She bought 5# @ 35¢/lb.

4. He borrowed $4,000.00 @ $8\frac{1}{4}$% interest.

5. Gus swam the 400 yd. freestyle in 4'20".

6. I changed the $100 bill into $10 bills.

7. Name the number shown by these tallies: |||| || .

8. AB = BC and AB = 12 ft., ∴ BC = 12 ft.

9. $100 \div 10 = 10$
    80 " " " 8
    60 " " " 6

Set Notation 65

Set Notation

Grouping Symbols
For mathematical parentheses, brackets and braces, see pages 44-49.

Signs of Comparison
In addition to those signs of comparison already presented, several comparison signs are commonly used in set notation in school mathematics.

Inclusion ("is contained in"; "is a proper subset of") $(\subset)$

$x \subset Y$

Bar under Inclusion ("is a subset of") $(\subseteq)$

$c \subseteq A$

Reverse Inclusion ("contains") $(\supset)$

$Y \supset x$

Membership ("belongs to"; "is an element of") $(\in)$

$3 \in$ set B

Vertical Bar ("such that") $(|)$

$\{n \mid 4 < n < 8\}$

"the set of all n such that n is greater than 4 and less than 8"

Note that the vertical bar may be a sign of grouping. (See page 48.) It may also be a sign of operation, but not in school mathematics.

Signs of Operation
Signs of operation require no space before or after the symbol.

Intersection (sign called *cap*) $(\cap)$

$A \cap B$

Union (sign called *cup*) $(\cup)$

$C \cup D$

Empty Set

The Empty Set $(\phi\ \phi)$

$(\{\ \})$

Follow the print in the choice of one or the other of these representations of the empty or null set.

⠲ ⠒ ⠰⠲ ⠈⠆ ⠐⠦ ⠰⠆ ⠒ ⠒⠒ ⠒⠒ ⠒⠒ ⠒⠒ $A \cup \emptyset = A$

⠒ ⠐⠖ ⠐⠂ ⠒⠒ ⠒⠒ ⠐⠒ ⠒⠒ ⠒⠒ ⠐⠒ ⠒⠰ ⠐⠖ ⠒⠒ ⠒⠒ ⠒⠰ ⠐⠂ ⠒⠒ ⠒⠒ ⠐⠖ ⠒⠒ ⠒⠒ ⠐⠖ ⠒⠒ ⠰⠆

⠒ ⠒ ⠒⠒ ⠒⠒ ⠰⠖ ⠒⠒ ⠒⠒ ⠰⠆ $\{1,\ 3,\ 5\} \cap \{2,\ 4,\ 6\} = \{\ \}$

For use of the NI within sets, see page 44.

Copy the examples on this and the previous page, and then transcribe these problems:

Practice Exercise

1. Let A = {1, 2, 3} and B = {a, b, c}. If C = the set of elements common to both A and B, C = $\emptyset$.

2. $1 \subset A$

3. $1 \not\subset B$

4. $c \in B$

5. A = B iff A $\subseteq$ B and B $\subseteq$ A. (iff means "if and only if")

6. $n(A \cup B \cup C) \neq n(D)$

7. C $\cup$ (A $\cap$ B)

8. Is 4 $\subseteq$ X if X = the set of all odd numbers?

9. {animals} $\supset$ {horses, cows, pigs}

10. $\{n \mid 12 > n > 2\}$

11. [Wed., Thurs., Fri.]

12. Paul $\in$ {people in the band}.

Rule XVI – Shapes

§ 106 Basic Shapes

A print mathematical shape is represented in braille by using the Shape Indicator, followed by a letter, a numeral, or a configuration of dots which is suggestive of the shape. Such a symbol is *not* used to replace the word or phrase which is the name of the shape.

Shape Indicator   □   ○   △

□   ∠   ⬡   ◯

§ 115 Spacing with Symbols of Shape

When a shape symbol is followed by its identification, such as a letter, sequence of letters, or numeral, there must be a space between the shape symbol and its identification. However, a shape symbol must be unspaced from any braille indicator or operation symbol which applies to it.

∠ 1

□ ABCD

In △ ABC, ∠ A = ?

∠ x + ∠ y

$$\triangle ABC$$
$$\triangle EFG$$

The combination of a sign of shape and its identification is considered one item in an "enclosed list."

(△ABC, △DEF)

(An "enclosed list" of two items.)

Some shapes are signs of comparison, and the braille symbols are spaced like other comparison symbols:

∥ is parallel to   ∦ is not parallel to

AB ∦ CD

⊥ is perpendicular to   ⊥̸ is not perpendicular to

AB ⊥ CD

Rule XVI – Shapes

Arrows as Signs of Comparison

⠿⠿ → right-pointing arrow, contracted form

⠿⠿⠿⠿ → right-pointing arrow, uncontracted form

⠿⠿⠿⠿ ← left-pointing arrow (never contracted)

These arrows indicate the relationship, "if ____ (the quantity at unbarbed end), then ____ (the quantity at barbed end)," or "____ implies ____." (Note spacing as symbols of comparison.)

⠿⠿⠿⠿⠿⠿ f→g "f implies g," or "if f, then g"

⠿⠿⠿⠿⠿⠿⠿⠿ f←g "f is implied by g," or "if g, then f"

The contracted right-pointing arrow is the one commonly used in the simple constructions of school mathematics. More complicated constructions of higher mathematics employ the uncontracted form, and the left-pointing arrow.

⠿⠿⠿⠿⠿ ↔ two-way horizontal arrow

This arrow is used to represent "has one-to-one correspondence with," "if and only if," and sometimes an infinite or "open" number line.

⠿⠿⠿⠿⠿⠿⠿⠿⠿⠿⠿⠿⠿⠿⠿⠿⠿⠿

Set A ↔ B. "Set A has one-to-one correspondence with Set B."

⠿⠿⠿⠿⠿⠿⠿⠿⠿⠿⠿⠿⠿⠿⠿⠿⠿⠿⠿⠿

X ⊃ y ↔ y > 0 "X contains y if and only if y is greater than zero."

Justify use and non-use of the ELI in these two examples.

For the many variations in arrow constructions that may be used in higher mathematics, see the Code Book, pages 145-51.

Copy all the examples above.

Rule XVI – Shapes

§ 115, b Shape Symbols That Represent Omission

Shape symbols are often used to indicate omission, as in $7 + \square = 12$. In formal transcription, a shape used for this purpose must be transcribed exactly and must be spaced in accordance with the omitted item which it represents.

⠿⠿⠿⠿⠿⠿⠿⠿⠿⠿ $2 + 4 \triangle 7$

(The triangle represents an omitted comparison sign.)

⠿⠿⠿⠿⠿⠿⠿⠿⠿⠿⠿⠿⠿ $x \square y = y \square x$

(The square represents an omitted sign of operation.)

⠿⠿⠿⠿⠿⠿⠿⠿⠿⠿⠿⠿⠿⠿⠿⠿⠿ $1 \text{ day} = 24$ ⬡

(The hexagon represents an omitted word or abbreviation.)

⠿⠿⠿⠿⠿⠿⠿⠿⠿⠿⠿ $3 \times 4 = \triangle$ ⠿⠿⠿⠿ $\square \%$

(The triangle and the square represent omitted numerals.)

There is no mathematical significance to any of the above shapes. Each example would be understood correctly if the general omission symbol were used, and in the classroom it would save time, space and effort to do so. On the other hand, in the following example the shapes are not signs of omission, but have mathematical significance, and must be transcribed exactly.

⠿⠿⠿⠿⠿⠿⠿⠿⠿⠿⠿⠿⠿⠿⠿⠿⠿⠿⠿⠿⠿⠿⠿⠿⠿⠿⠿⠿⠿⠿⠿⠿⠿⠿⠿⠿

⠿⠿⠿⠿⠿⠿⠿⠿⠿⠿⠿⠿ This numeration system uses the symbols, $\triangle, \square, \square$.

Note the PI in this example. It must precede punctuation that follows a shape symbol.

Rule XXIII, § 177 viii Use of Multipurpose Indicator with Regular Polygons

A regular polygon whose shape symbol includes a number (square, hexagon, octagon, etc.) may be used to represent omission of a symbol of operation. When such a shape symbol is followed by a numeral, the multipurpose indicator, dot 5, must precede the numeral. Check the examples to see why.

⠿⠿⠿⠿⠿⠿⠿⠿⠿⠿⠿⠿⠿⠿ $18 = 5 \square 13$

⠿⠿⠿⠿⠿ ⠿⠿ ⠿⠿⠿ n ⬡ $6 = 6n$

Copy the examples above.

70 **Rule XVI – Shapes**

§ 114 Plural of a Sign of Shape
The plural or possessive of a sign of shape may be indicated in print by an *s* inside the shape, or after it. In braille, the *s* (uncapitalized) is written immediately after the shape symbol. In the case of a possessive, follow the print as to use or non-use of an apostrophe.

⠿⠀⠿⠀⠿   Ⓢ   ⠿⠀⠿⠀⠿⠀⠿⠀⠿   □'s

§ 27, b The ELI and Shapes
The ELI is not used with a "single letter" or "short-form combination":

1. that follows a symbol of shape if the symbol of shape does not have a plural or possessive ending.

⠿⠀⠿⠀⠿⠀⠿   ∠ a

2. that precedes or follows a symbol of shape representing omission.

⠿⠀⠿⠀⠿⠀⠿⠀⠿⠀⠿   a △ b (△ represents a comparison sign.)

(See also the second example on page 69, in which the shape represents an omitted sign of operation.)

⠿⠀⠿

Find the sum of the n ∠ 's.

The ELI is required because the shape sign for *angle* is not an omission sign.

For other shapes, and for transcription of shaded or filled-in shapes, see the Code Book, pages 110-118.

Practice Exercise
Transcribe the following problems:

1. ∠ BAC + ∠ ABC = ∠ ACB

2. $\frac{□}{○}$ (Transcribe in both linear and spatial arrangements.)

3. $a \leftrightarrow 1, b \leftrightarrow 2, c \leftrightarrow 3$

4. Give the formula for finding the area of a circle.

5. If MN ∥ RS, and RS ∥ XY, is MN ∥ XY?

6. Set A = {△, □, ○}

7. ⧌ ABC and DEF are congruent.

8. n □ 4 = 12

9. If △ = 5 and □ = 10, what is the value of △□?

Rule XIII – Superscripts and Subscripts

§ 71 Definition of Terms
The normal level of writing is called the "base line." Some mathematical expressions employ signs, usually in smaller type than the normal, which are written above or below the base line. A sign which is elevated is called a "superscript," as in x^2; one which is lowered is called a "subscript," as in y_1. A change to either of these levels must be shown by the use of the appropriate indicator, and the return to the base line must be shown by the use of the base-line indicator unless it is indicated in one of the other ways presented below (§ 79).

§ 73 Level Indicators
Base-line ⠐ (dot 5); Superscript ⠘; Subscript ⠰

⠐⠦⠬ x^2 ⠐⠦⠬⠼⠰ x^2y ⠦⠰⠁ x_a (x sub a)   ⠝⠰⠤⠆ n_{-2}

§ 75 Left Superscripts and Subscripts
Superscripts and subscripts are also found to the left of base-line expressions. In such cases, the appropriate level indicator appears first in the expression, then the superscript or subscript symbol, then the base-line indicator, and finally the symbol on the base line with which the superscript or subscript is associated. Such formations are not common in school mathematics, however.

⠘⠦⠐⠝ $^x n$ ⠰⠉⠐⠽ $_c y$ ⠘⠤⠐⠭ $^- x$ (the additive inverse of x; one common left superscript)

§ 72 Hierarchy of Superscripts and Subscripts
Superscripts or subscripts only one level removed from the base line, as in x^2 and y_1, are "of the first order." These superscripts or subscripts may carry superscripts or subscripts of their own, which are referred to as superscripts or subscripts "of the second order:" x_{2_r}; y^{n^2}. If those of the second order also carry superscripts or subscripts, these are "of the third order." A higher order is rare, though possible. The transcription of superscripts and subscripts beyond the first order is discussed and illustrated on pages 84-86 of the Code Book.

§ 77 Numeric Subscripts
Right numeric subscripts of first order only, associated with an abbreviated function name or a letter which has a separate identity, are written without a subscript indicator. The letter may be modified by one or more primes, or a superscript, but the subscript must carry no superscripts or subscripts of its own, and must consist of numeric symbols only.

⠭⠼⠁ x_1 ⠽⠄⠼⠁ y'_1 ⠭⠄⠄⠼⠆ x''_2

Note that a prime is not a superscript.

⠝⠼⠁⠼⠚⠂⠚⠚⠚ $n_{10,000}$ ⠇⠕⠛⠼⠆⠐⠭ $\log_2 x$

Rule XIII – Superscripts and Subscripts

The base-line indicator is not needed after these subscripts in which no subscript indicator is used.

⠿ ⠿ ⠿ ⠿ ⠿ ⠿ $(a_2 + 1)$

In order to distinguish between this form and a2 (the 2 on the base line), the multipurpose indicator, dot 5, is used between the *a* and the 2.

⠿ ⠿ ⠿   a2

In contrast to the examples just given, the following constructions require the use of the subscript indicator. In each case, decide why this is so. Which condition(s) required for omission of the subscript indicator is not met? (See pages 86-88, Code Book.)

⠿ ⠿ ⠿ ⠿ $_3x$ ⠿ ⠿ ⠿ ⠿ ⠿ 12_7 ⠿ ⠿ ⠿ ⠿ $x_{2'}$

⠿ ⠿ ⠿ ⠿ ⠿ x_{2+k} ⠿ ⠿ ⠿ ⠿ ⠿ ⠿ ⠿ $seven_3$

Rule XXIII, § 177, iii Use of Multipurpose Indicator with Subscript

The Multipurpose Indicator, dot 5, must be used between a numeric subscript and a numeral which follows it on the base line.

⠿ ⠿ ⠿ ⠿ ⠿ ⠿ ⠿ ⠿ ⠿ ⠿ ⠿ ⠿ ⠿ ⠿ ⠿ ⠿ ⠿ ⠿ ⠿ $C_0 10^2 + C_1 10 + C_2$

§ 79 Changes of Level

It is easy to forget to use the base-line indicator after a superscript or subscript to bring the work back to normal base-line level, but this indicator must be used unless the previous indicator is cancelled by one of these other possible circumstances, which all reinstate the base-line level:

1. The PI follows the superscript or subscript.

⠿   ⠿ ⠿ ⠿ ⠿ ⠿ ⠿

Find the value of x^3. $x^{2'}s$

2. A comma follows the superscript or subscript.

⠿ ⠿ ⠿ ⠿ ⠿ ⠿ ⠿ ⠿ x^2, x^3

A comma within a long numeral does not have the same effect.

⠿ ⠿ ⠿ ⠿ ⠿ ⠿ ⠿ ⠿ ⠿ ⠿ ⠿ $x^{16,000} + ?$

Copy the examples on this page.

Rule XIII – Superscripts and Subscripts

73

3. A space or transition to a new line comes after the superscript or subscript and is followed by literary text, unrelated mathematical material, or a comparison symbol.

⠿⠿⠿⠿⠿⠿⠿⠿⠿⠿⠿⠿⠿⠿⠿⠿⠿⠿⠿ $2p^2$ is always even.

(Space, followed by literary text.)

⠿⠿⠿⠿⠿⠿⠿⠿⠿⠿⠿⠿⠿ $2^x < 3^x$

(Space, followed by comparison symbol.)

⠿⠿⠿⠿⠿⠿⠿ ⠿⠿ ⠿⠿⠿⠿ ⠿⠿ ⠿⠿⠿⠿⠿⠿ ⠿⠿

⠿⠿⠿⠿ ⠿⠿⠿ ⠿⠿⠿⠿⠿⠿ ⠿⠿⠿⠿⠿⠿⠿

⠿⠿ ⠿⠿⠿⠿⠿⠿⠿⠿⠿⠿⠿⠿⠿⠿⠿⠿⠿⠿⠿⠿⠿

⠿⠿⠿⠿⠿⠿⠿⠿⠿

Conversion of a base 5 numeral to a base 10 numeral: $2341_5 = 2 \cdot 5^3 + 3 \cdot 5^2 + 4 \cdot 5^1 + 1 \cdot 5^0$.

Assuming lines short enough to require division as above, the third line begins with a comparison symbol which reinstates the base-line level. The last runover does not begin with a comparison symbol, so a base-line indicator is needed before the plus sign.

4. A space after a symbol of shape, an abbreviated function name, or an unabbreviated function name in mathematical context, preserves the level already in effect; but if these items carry a superscript or subscript, the space following it reinstates the level that was in effect before.

⠿⠿⠿⠿⠿⠿⠿ $\cos^2 x$ The space reinstates the level of *cos*.

⠿⠿⠿⠿⠿⠿⠿⠿⠿⠿⠿ $b_{\triangle ABC}$

In this case, ABC is part of the subscript, and the space following the shape symbol does not reinstate base-line level. (See Code Book, page 91.)

In most other cases, return to the base-line must be shown by use of the base-line indicator. See pages 89-92 of the Code Book for further rules and examples.

⠿⠿⠿⠿⠿⠿ $x^2 + 1$ ⠿⠿⠿⠿⠿⠿⠿⠿ $\dfrac{1}{x^2}$

⠿⠿⠿⠿⠿⠿⠿⠿⠿⠿⠿ $(x^2 + y^2)$

Copy the examples on this page.

74   **Rule XIII – Superscripts and Subscripts**

5. Contractions may not be used in a word or abbreviation in contact with a level indicator.

⠿ ⠿ ⠿ ⠿ ⠿ ⠿ ⠿ ⠿ ⠿ 13_{seven}

⠿ ⠿ ⠿ ⠿ ⠿ ⠿ ⠿ ⠿ ⠿ ⠿   inch-pound^2

The small hollow dot used in print as the sign for "degrees" is a superscript. The braille

symbol is   ⠿ ⠿

⠿ $90° + 90° = ?°$

Copy the examples above.

Practice Exercise
Transcribe the following problems.

1. This quantity is the equivalent of x^2.

2. $b^{-2} = \dfrac{1}{b^2}$

3. a_2, b_2

4. a^2 means a $\times$ a.

5. $y^2 - x_a$

6. At sea level, water boils at 212° F.

7. $27_{ten} = 123_{four}$

8. $[(a^2 + b^2)(x + y)^2]$

9. $\pi r^2 =$ the _____ of a circle. (See page 36 for Greek letter.)

Rule XIV – Modifiers   75

Rule XIV – Modifiers

§ 85 Modifiers

A modifier is a superscript or subscript placed directly over or directly under a mathematical expression. Modifiers include arcs, arrows, bars, dots, tildes, and other forms. See pages 97-99, Code Book.

§ 86 Modified Expressions

Modified expressions are transcribed according to a five-step rule outlined on page 99 of the Code Book, using several indicators:

⠐⠂ Multipurpose Indicator   ⠨⠲ Directly-Over Indicator

⠠⠢ Directly-Under Indicator   ⠐⠆ Termination Indicator

A step-by-step transcription of a simple modification is shown below.

To transcribe the print representation of a line segment, $\overline{AC}$:

1. The multipurpose indicator prepares the reader for a modifier.

2. The expression to be modified follows the multipurpose indicator.

3. The appropriate modification indicator, "directly-over" or "directly-under," follows the expression being modified.

4. The modifier symbol follows the modification indicator. The symbol in this example is the horizontal bar, dots 1-5-6.

5. The termination indicator signifies the completion of the modified expression.

Such a modified expression may never be divided at the end of a line.

Using the pattern just presented, transcribe the modified expression $\overset{\frown}{EF}$.

The symbol for the concave upward arc is

Rule XIV – Modifiers

Look at examples (1) through (7), pages 99 and 100 and (1) through (3), page 105, Code Book and analyze the composition of each, naming each configuration. Copy these examples.

The bar over the function name *limit* (or *lim*) is not treated as a modifier. See Code Book, page 120, § 118 for transcription of this term.

§ 86, b Contracted Form of Modification

A single digit or letter modified by a horizontal bar directly over it is expressed simply by transcribing the digit or letter, followed by the bar. This contracted form is used whenever possible.

⠿ ⠿ $\bar{x}$ ⠿ ⠿ ⠿ ⠿ $\overline{xyz}$ ⠿ ⠿ ⠿ ⠿ $\bar{x}^2$

Analyze all the examples on pages 100 and 101, Section 86, b, Code Book.

§ 97, b and 99, a Recurring Digits in Decimal Numbers

The horizontal bar and the dot are both used in print to indicate the recurrence of one or more digits in a decimal numeral. The bar is extended over all the digits which recur, in print or in braille. The dot is repeated, in print, over each digit of the recurring sequence, but in braille a single dot is used to modify a decimal numeral. The braille symbol for the dot is 1-6.

⠿ ⠿ ⠿ ⠿ $.\bar{3}$ (contracted modifier)   ⠿ ⠿ ⠿ ⠿ ⠿ ⠿ ⠿ ⠿ ⠿ ⠿ $.\overline{7128}$

⠿ ⠿ ⠿ ⠿ ⠿ ⠿ ⠿ ⠿ ⠿ ⠿ ⠿ $3.57\overline{29}$ ⠿ ⠿ ⠿ ⠿ ⠿ ⠿ ⠿ ⠿ $.\dot{3}$

⠿ ⠿ ⠿ ⠿ ⠿ ⠿ ⠿ ⠿ ⠿ $.13\dot{5}$ ⠿ ⠿ ⠿ ⠿ ⠿ ⠿ ⠿ ⠿ ⠿ $.1\dot{3}\dot{5}$

Configurations other than recurring decimals which include superscribed dots must be transcribed with as many dots as are shown in the printed text.

⠿ ⠿ ⠿ ⠿ ⠿ ⠿ $\ddot{x}$

Rule IX § 55, a, vi Contractions in Modified Words

Contractions may not be used in a word or abbreviation that is in contact with any modifier symbol.

⠿ ⠿ ⠿ ⠿ ⠿ ⠿ ⠿ ⠿ ⠿ ⠿ ⠿ $\underset{\longrightarrow}{heat}$

The PI must be used before punctuation that follows a modified expression.

⠿ ⠿ ⠿   ⠿ ⠿ ⠿ ⠿ ⠿   ⠿ ⠿   ⠿ ⠿ ⠿ ⠿ ⠿ ⠿   One ninth = $.\bar{1}$.

Copy the examples on this page.

Rule XIV – Modifiers

Practice Exercise
Transcribe the following problems:

1. $\overline{x^2}$

2. $\overrightarrow{MN}$

3. $\overline{(a + b)}$

4. $\overline{x}'s$

5. $\dfrac{2}{3} = .\dot{6}$

6. $\overline{(\overline{m^2} + \overline{n^2})}$

Try this one, after reading the instructions under it in parentheses:

7. $C + O_2 \xrightarrow{\triangle} CO_2$ Carbon plus oxygen, in the presence of heat, yields carbon dioxide.

(In this transcription, $\triangle$ is the modifier. It is the upper-case Greek letter *delta*. See page 36 for its transcription. Treat the arrow as a sign of comparison.)

Now transcribe this sentence:

8. "In the presence of heat" is represented by $\xrightarrow{\triangle}$

Rule XV – Radicals

§ 103 Simple Radicals
The most common radical is the square root. To transcribe the square root of a quantity shown within the usual print sign ($\sqrt{}$), write the radical symbol, then the quantity (the "radicand"), then the termination indicator:

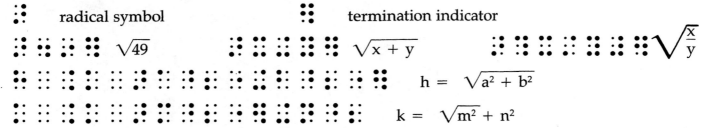

§ 104 Index of Radical
If an index of the radical is shown in print, the transcription begins with the index-of-radical indicator, followed by the index numeral, then the radical symbol, the radicand, and the termination indicator.

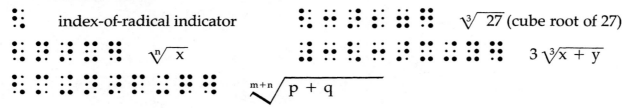

Rule IX, § 55, a, vii Contractions in Radicals
Contractions may not be used in a word or abbreviation that is in contact with the radical symbol.

⠀⠀⠀⠀⠀⠀⠀ $\sqrt{\text{eight}}$

§ 181 Spatial Arrangement of a Square-Root Problem
See Code Book, pages 177 and 178, for two examples of square-root problems in spatial arrangement.

§ 105 Nested Radicals
For transcription of radicals within radicals ("nested"), see pages 109 and 110, Code Book.

Copy the examples above and then transcribe these problems.

Practice Exercise

1. $\sqrt{25}$

2. $\sqrt{a-b}$

3. $\sqrt{\frac{1}{4} + \frac{1}{3}}$

4. $\sqrt[3]{x^3} + y^3$

5. $\sqrt{\text{sixteen}}$

6. $-\sqrt{4} = -2$

Rule XXV – Format

Pages 184 through 207 of the Code Book give detailed rules and illustrative examples for formats used in transcribing many types of mathematical problems. The following topics are included:

1. Numbering or lettering of spatial arrangements on a page, starting with § 185, b, page 184, and continuing through page 188. Note especially the placement of numbers before division problems, page 186, ii.

2. Keying technique, sometimes needed in transcribing tables, matrices, etc., pages 188-190.

3. Definitions, transcription formats, and numbering of "displayed," "embedded," and "linked" expressions, pages 190-192.

4. Margins for narrative portions of text, pages 192-193.

5. Margins and numbering of spatial non-itemized materials, pages 193-198.

6. Margins and numbering of spatial itemized materials, pages 199-201.

7. Tabular materials, pages 201-203.

8. Format for formal proofs, pages 204-205.

9. Runovers, pages 206-207. Some of the rules concerning runovers are included on the next two pages, for ease in reference.

§ 195 Runovers

The runover of a mathematical expression to another braille line should be avoided if possible.

> NOTE: A mathematical expression can consist of one letter or one numeral or of a long string of letters, numerals, operation signs, comparison signs, words and other material which makes a mathematical statement.

1. It is preferable to leave part of another line blank if that will keep all of a mathematical expression on one line.

We can show that if a = b, then for all values of c, ac = bc.
(a = b, c, and ac = bc are all mathematical expressions.)

2. A sequence of mathematical expressions which occurs in an "enclosed list" must not be divided between braille lines if all of the list can be kept on a single braille line by adjusting the spacing of the surrounding material.

The elements of the sequence (10, 11, 12, 13, ... , 19) can be counted.

Copy the two examples above, dividing lines exactly as shown.

3. An abbreviation must not be placed on a different braille line from its preceding or following numeral or letter.

    4 in   30° C

    x ft.   fig. 7

4. A hyphenated expression in which one component of the expression is mathematical must not be divided between braille lines.

    4-sided figure

    x-intercept

Identify the separate mathematical expressions on this page.

Rule XXV – Format

5. When a mathematical expression *must* be divided between lines, the division must be made giving priority to the following items in descending order:

   i. After a comma which occurs between items in an "enclosed list."

   ii. Before a symbol of comparison.

   iii. Before a symbol of operation.

   iv. Before a fraction line.

   v. Before the base-line indicator.

   vi. Before a change-of-level indicator or within a superscript or subscript before one of the symbols listed above.

   vii. Between factors which are enclosed within grouping symbols.

   viii. After a termination indicator.

If an expression must be divided at an item lower on the priority list, it must also be divided at <u>each</u> item appearing higher on the list.

Cumulative Lists of Rules

In order to achieve a sequential presentation throughout this manual, it has been necessary to present the use of some Nemeth symbols and rules in piecemeal fashion, a few applications at a time. In the following section, all the rules presented throughout the manual on the more complicated topics are pulled together for review and easy reference. These rules are stated briefly, but the number of the page on which each was originally presented is given in parentheses, so that the student may refer back to that page for further explanation and illustration.

Refer to Appendix B in the Code Book to locate and identify either print signs or braille symbols which do not appear in this book. This Appendix contains a listing of all Nemeth Symbols in the standard order for braille.

The Numeric Indicator

A. USE the Numeric Indicator before a numeral:
1. at the beginning of a braille line or after a space (2)
2. at the beginning of the new line in the runover of a divided long numeral (3)
3. after a minus symbol occurring at the beginning of a braille line or after a space (4)
4. after a space in a fraction arranged spatially (18)
5. after a mark of punctuation (31)
6. after a hyphen that follows a word, abbreviation, or mark of punctuation (32, 42)
7. before the decimal point in a decimal numeral in the same circumstances as 1, 2, etc., above (3)

B. DO NOT USE the Numeric Indicator before a numeral:
1. in a problem arranged spatially for computation (5)
2. after a hyphen that follows a mathematical expression (32)
3. which is an item in an "enclosed list" (44)
4. at the beginning of a new line in the runover of a divided "enclosed list" (45)

The Punctuation Indicator

A. USE the Punctuation Indicator before punctuation that follows:
1. any braille indicator (26)
2. any mathematical symbol written as in the Nemeth Code (26) (This includes "single letters.") (36)
3. a Roman numeral (26)
4. a dash or ellipsis in math context (27)
5. a sequence of letters, each having separate identity (not an abbreviation) (27)
6. ordinal endings (27)
7. the apostrophe-s combination in plural or possessive endings, and also *before* the apostrophe in these endings (27)

Cumulative Lists of Rules 83

    8. any abbreviated function name, or any unabbreviated function name in mathematical context (28)

    9. the general omission symbol (33)

   10. a grouping symbol (49)

   11. a symbol of comparison (61)

   12. any of the miscellaneous symbols of Rule XXII (63)

   13. any symbol of shape (69)

   14. any modified expression (76)

There are a few other circumstances in which the PI is required, but they occur very rarely.

See Code Book, § 37, for a complete listing.

B. DO NOT USE the Punctuation Indicator before punctuation:

    1. at the beginning of a braille line or after a space (29)

    2. after a numeric symbol written as in English (literary) Braille (29)

    3. after a dash or ellipsis in literary context (29)

    4. after a word or abbreviation (29, 41)

    5. before a comma, hyphen, dash, or ellipsis (30)

The English-Letter Indicator

A. USE the English-Letter Indicator:

    1. before a "single letter" or "short-form combination" (36), except as indicated below

    2. before all lower-case Roman numerals (With an upper-case Roman numeral of only one letter, follow ELI usage as for any letter.) (38)

    3. with single lower-case letters in diagrams (39)

    4. with an abbreviation consisting of one letter, or letters forming a short-form word, if not followed by a period which applies to the abbreviation (41)

B. DO NOT USE the ELI:

    1. with a "single letter" or "short-form combination"

      a. that follows a function name or its abbreviation (37)

      b. that is preceded or followed by a comparison symbol (38)

      c. that is an abbreviation and is followed by a period which applies to it (41)

      d. that is an item in an "enclosed list" (45)

      e. that follows a sign of shape, or precedes a sign of shape representing omission (70)

    2. with single capital letters in diagrams (39)

    3. before a letter or combination of unspaced letters in direct contact with both an opening and a closing grouping symbol (If such letters are in contact with only one of the grouping symbols, follow ELI usage as if the grouping symbols were not there.) (46)

Contractions

A. USE contractions *except* in words or abbreviations that immediately precede or follow these Nemeth symbols.

1. braille indicators except capitalization indicators or the italic sign of English Braille (50)
2. the general omission symbol (50)
3. any operation symbol (50)
4. any comparison symbol, even though a space precedes or follows it (51)
5. any modifier symbol (76)
6. the radical symbol (78)

B. Never use contractions in abbreviated function names, nor unabbreviated function names in mathematical context. (52)

C. Do not use contractions in abbreviations preceding the symbols listed under *A*, above, unless a period which applies to the abbreviation intervenes. (52) In the abbreviation *in* or *in.* for *inch* or *inches*, the contraction for *in* is never used. The only abbreviations in which the *st* contraction may be used are those for *street* or *saint*. (53)

D. The contractions for *to, into,* and *by* are restricted as in *A*, above, and in addition must not be used before: (See F below.)

1. any word or abbreviation in which contractions may not be used (54)
2. any abbreviation consisting of only one letter or of a short-form combination (54)
3. a Roman numeral (55)
4. a Nemeth numeric symbol (55)
5. a dash or ellipsis (55)
6. a "single letter" (55)
7. a sequence of mathematical letters (55)
8. an abbreviated function name, or an unabbreviated function name in mathematical context (55)
9. a grouping symbol (55)

E. The *st* and *th* contractions are not used for ordinal endings attached to numerals, letters, or other mathematical expressions. (56)

F. Whole-word alphabet contractions and whole-word lower sign contactions must not be used in contact with any grouping symbol. *Enough, were* and *into* may be partially contracted. (57)

G. The contractions for *and, for, of, the, with,* as either whole or part words, must not be used in direct contact with any grouping symbol, and when they may not be used as part words because of this rule, no other contractions may be used in the words affected. They *may* be used, in a word which is in contact with a grouping symbol, if the contraction itself is not in contact with the grouping symbol. (57)

Cumulative Lists of Rules

H. Contractions are used in words or abbreviations which are in contact with grouping symbols unless limiting factors listed above are present. (58)

I. Contractions must not be used when they could be mistaken for mathematical expressions. (58)

The Multipurpose Indicator

A. USE the Multipurpose Indicator:

1. in writing the remainder in a division problem (15)

2. between a tally mark and the PI (63)

3. between the shape symbol for a regular polygon, used to represent omission of a symbol of operation, and a numeral which follows it (69)

4. between a letter and an unspaced succeeding numeral to indicate that the numeral is not a subscript to the letter (72)

5. between a numeric subscript and a numeral which is on the base line (72)

6. as the first symbol of a modified expression (75)

ANSWER SECTION

This section contains braille answers to the problems presented as Practice Exercises, beginning with those on the second line of the exercise on page 2.

Practice Exercises on Pages 2, 3, and 4

Page 2

Page 3

Page 4

Practice Exercise on Page 6

Page 6

90 Practice Exercises on Pages 7 and 9

Page 7

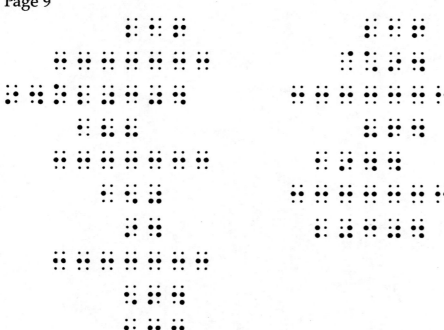

Page 9

Practice Exercise on Page 9 (cont'd.) 91

Page 9 (cont'd.)

Page 10

Practice Exercise on Page 11

Page 11

Page 14

Practice Exercises on Pages 15, 16, and 17

Page 15

Page 16

Page 17

Page 18

Page 23

In this example, in which one problem must be broken into three segments, the entire problem is interpreted as the "over-all arrangement." The extra cell required at the end of a separation line is placed at the very end of the problem.

Practice Exercise on Page 25

97

Page 25

Page 28

Practice Exercises on Pages 30 and 31

Page 30

Page 31

Page 32

Practice Exercise on Page 32 (cont'd.)

Page 32 (cont'd.)

Page 34

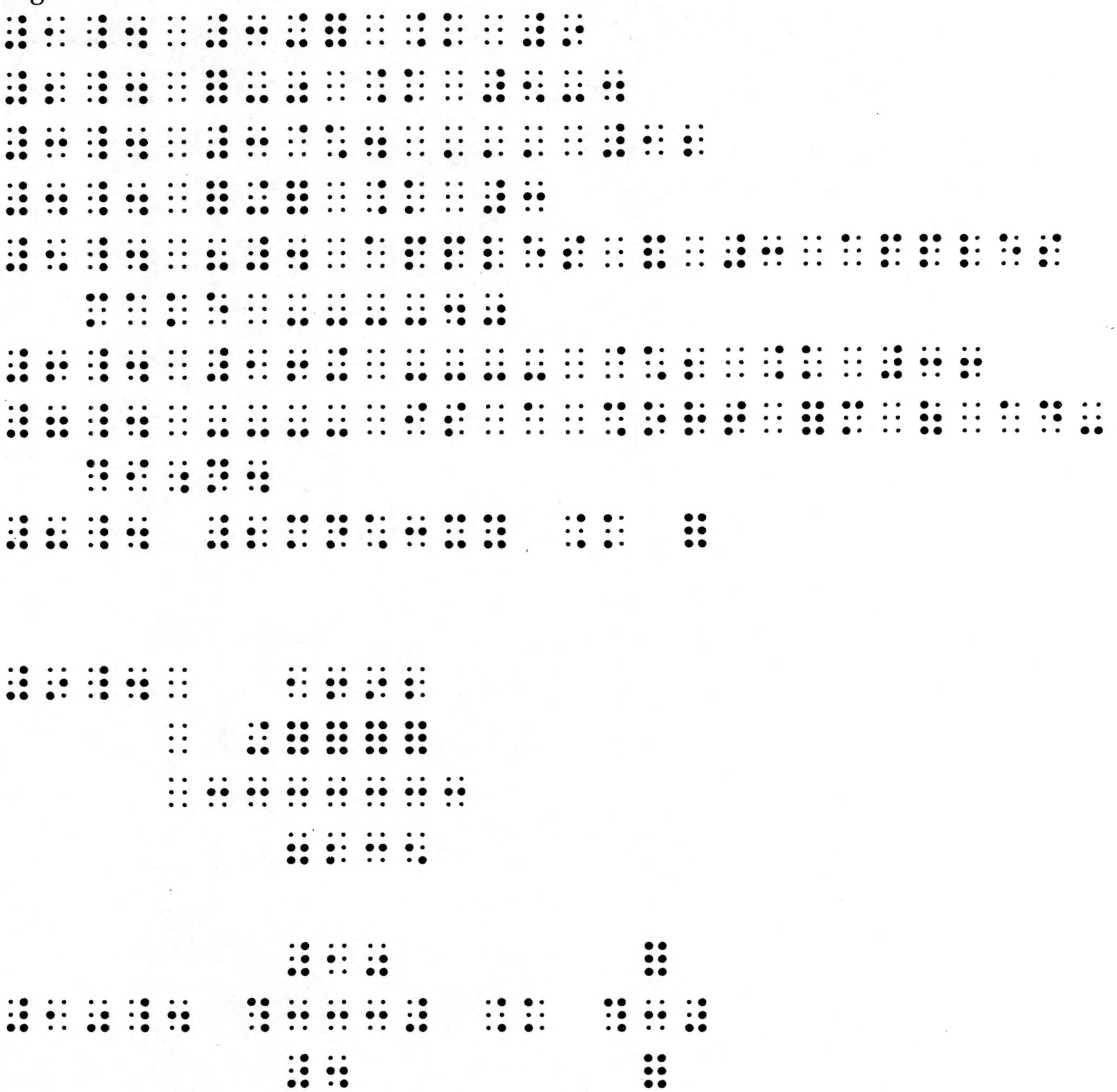

Practice Exercise on Page 39

Page 39

Practice Exercises on Pages 40 and 42

Page 40

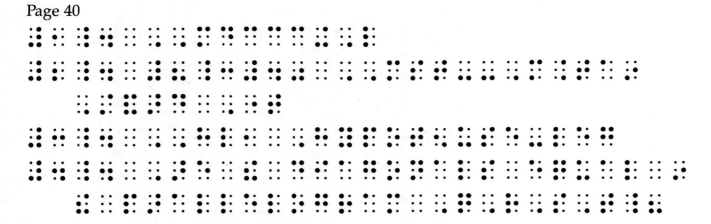

Page 42

Question after 4th example on page: Because there is no period after the F, we may assume that there would be none after the C if it did not end the sentence.

Practice Exercise on Page 43

Page 43

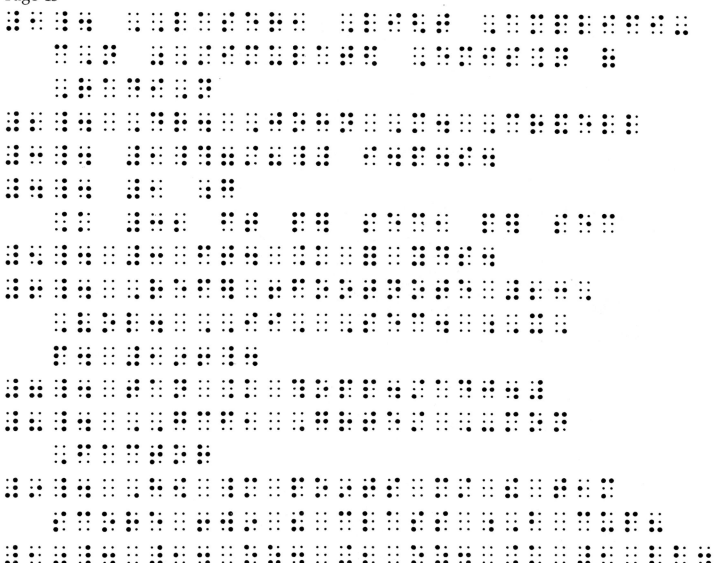

Page 47

An "enclosed list"

Not an "enclosed list" because of comparison signs

No ELI's because of comparison signs

Not an "enclosed list" because only one item within grouping symbols

No ELI because the one letter is in contact with both opening and closing grouping symbols

Not an "enclosed list" because items not separated by commas

No ELI because *n* not followed by a space or punctuation so is not a "single letter"

No NI's because numerals not preceded by a space

Not an "enclosed list" because of semicolon

ELI's because each item is a "single letter"

Not an "enclosed list" because of ordinal endings

No NI before *1st* because not preceded by a space

An "enclosed list"

No ELI's with letters following an abbreviated function name

An "enclosed list," therefore no NI's at beginnings of items

An "enclosed list," therefore no NI's

An "enclosed list," therefore no ELI's

Practice Exercise on Page 47 (cont'd.)

Page 47 (cont'd.)

Not an "enclosed list" because of semicolon

No NI before first item because not preceded by a space

Not an "enclosed list" because not two items separated by commas, therefore ignore the grouping signs

If the sign between the two letters is a hyphen, both are "single letters" and require ELI's. If the sign is a minus sign, neither is a "single letter" and no ELI's should be used.

An "enclosed list," therefore no ELI's

Not an "enclosed list" because words included, not two items, no commas

ELI because x is a "single letter"

Not an "enclosed list" because consists of abbreviations

No ELI before g because followed by a period which applies to it

Not an "enclosed list" because of words

No ELI before A because followed by a comparison symbol

Not an "enclosed list" because of apostrophes

No NI before 3 because not preceded by a space

No ELI before s because in contact with both opening and closing grouping symbols

Practice Exercises on Pages 49 and 51

Page 49

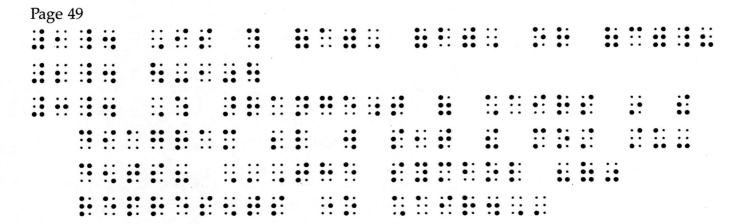

Page 51, last example

1. *Journey* limited by equals sign.
2. *Distance* and *used* limited by fraction indicators.
3. *Amount* limited by fraction line (a symbol of operation). *Traveled* is limited by fraction line.

Practice Exercise on Page 54

Page 54

⠿ (braille)

Contract *ong* because followed by period which intervenes between the contraction and the = symbol.

⠿ (braille)

No limiting factors present

⠿ (braille)

Contractions not used in function names in mathematical context (See Code Book, p.122, (4), to verify spacing in this example.)

⠿ (braille)

days not contracted because precedes equals sign

ELI with *yr* because it is an abbreviation which is a "short-form combination" and there is no period which applies to it.

⠿ (braille)

No limiting factors present

⠿ (braille)

ELI with *yr* because it is an abbreviation which is a "short-form combination" and there is no period which applies to it. No limiting factors for *days*.

⠿ (braille)

Never contract *in* for *inches*

Space must separate abbreviation and symbol of operation

⠿ (braille)

Contractions in both words limited by the division symbol

time would also be limited by the equals sign

⠿ (braille)

No contractions allowed in abbreviated function names

⠿ (braille)

Both words with possible contractions are in contact with the general omission symbol

Page 54, (cont'd.)

st contracted in abbreviation for *street* or *saint* only

ELI before "single letter"

Contractions not permitted in acronyms.

children followed by a comparison sign; others unlimited

horsepower precedes equals symbol

force, *distance* and *time* in contact with symbols of operation

time no longer in contact with a symbol of operation

hypotenuse and *the* limited by the equals symbol

Practice Exercise on Page 56

Page 56

⠿ ⠿ ⠿ ⠿ ⠿ ⠿ ⠿ ⠿ ⠿ ⠿ ⠿ ⠿ ⠿ ⠿ ⠿ ⠿ ⠿ ⠿ ⠿

in may not be contracted, therefore *to* may not be contracted

⠿ ⠿

by limited by ellipsis

⠿ ⠿

by limited by "single letter"

⠿ ⠿ ⠿ ⠿   ⠿ ⠿ ⠿ ⠿ ⠿   ⠿ ⠿ ⠿ ⠿ ⠿ ⠿
⠿ ⠿ ⠿ ⠿ ⠿ ⠿ ⠿ ⠿ ⠿   ⠿ ⠿   ⠿ ⠿ ⠿ ⠿ ⠿ ⠿

distance limited by fraction line; note that transition to a new line does not change this limitation.

store in contact with fraction indicator

to not contracted before uncontracted *store*

⠿ ⠿ ⠿ ⠿ ⠿ ⠿ ⠿ ⠿ ⠿ ⠿ ⠿ ⠿ ⠿ ⠿ ⠿ ⠿ ⠿ ⠿

to limited by Roman numeral

⠿ ⠿ ⠿ ⠿   ⠿ ⠿ ⠿ ⠿   ⠿ ⠿ ⠿   ⠿ ⠿ ⠿ ⠿   ⠿ ⠿ ⠿ ⠿ ⠿ ⠿ ⠿ ⠿
⠿ ⠿   ⠿ ⠿ ⠿ ⠿   ⠿ ⠿   ⠿ ⠿ ⠿
⠿ ⠿   ⠿

by limited by grouping symbol

No NI's in "enclosed lists"

⠿ ⠿

to limited by one-letter abbreviation

No ELI when abbreviation followed by period which applies to it. Since *oz* is followed by a period it may be assumed that the period after *g* applies to it.

⠿ ⠿
⠿ ⠿ ⠿ ⠿ ⠿ ⠿ ⠿ ⠿ ⠿ ⠿ ⠿ ⠿ ⠿ ⠿ ⠿ ⠿ ⠿ ⠿ ⠿ ⠿

to limited by abbreviated function name

⠿ ⠿

to limited by "single letter"

Page 56 (cont'd.)

into limited by Nemeth numeral

by limited by Nemeth numeral

min may be contracted

to limited by mark of punctuation, as in English Braille

to limited by sequence of letters, each with separate identity

to limited by Nemeth numeral

Practice Exercise on Page 59

Page 59

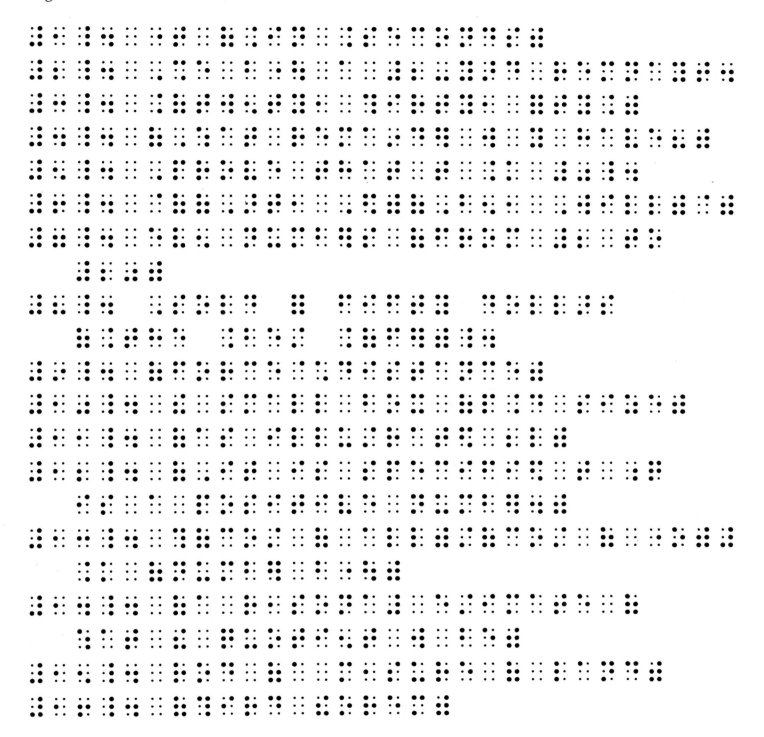

Page 61

Practice Exercise on Page 64

Page 64

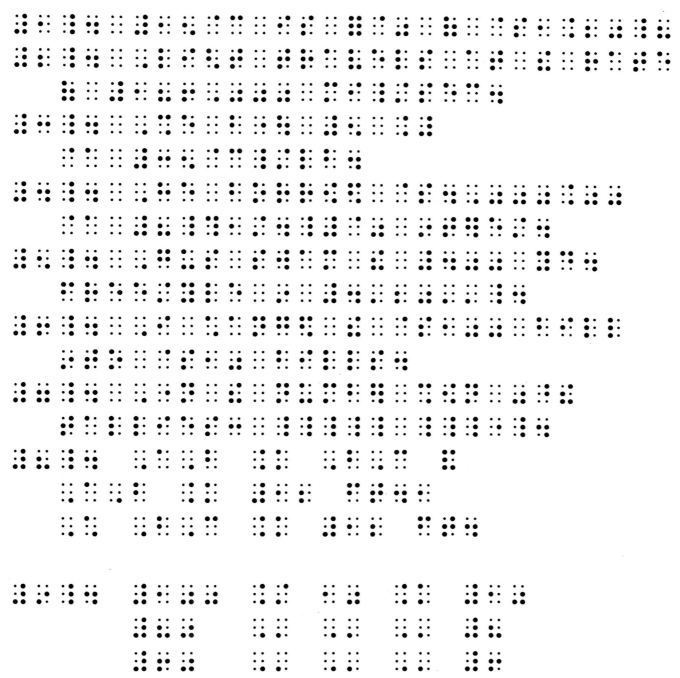

Notice the adjustments in spacing in the first line of 9, made in order to accommodate the ditto marks correctly. Also notice the left adjustment of the numerals in lines 2 and 3.

Page 66

Practice Exercise on Page 70 117

Page 70

Page 74

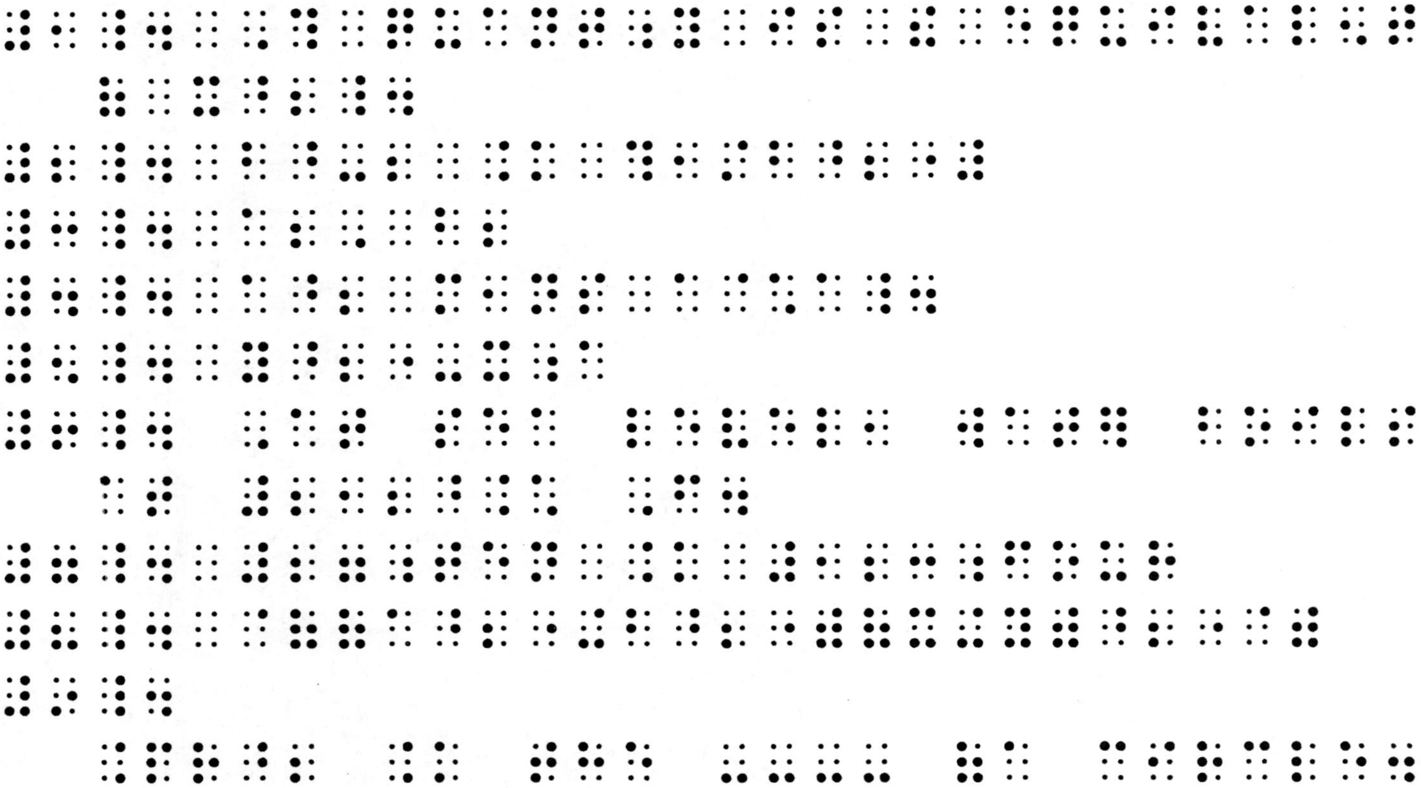

Page 77

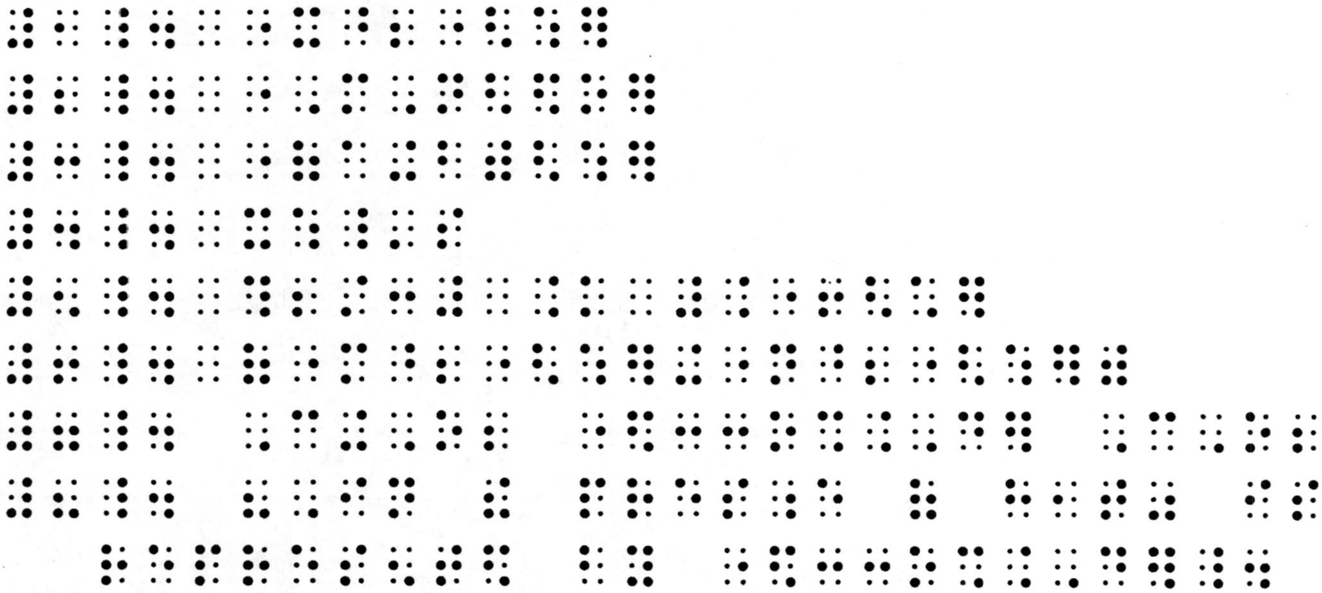

Practice Exercise on Page 78

Page 78

Index

Abbreviations, 41-43; measurement, 41; English-Letter Indicator with, 41-42; spacing with, 42; of reference, 42; contractions in, 52-53

Absolute value (Vertical bars), 48

Addition, 4-6; carried numbers in, 6; of fractions and mixed numbers, 19-20

Alphabetic Indicators, 36-39; Greek-Letter Indicator, 36; English-Letter Indicator, 36-39. *See also separate headings below*

Angles, 67-70

Apostrophe, 27; in dates, 29; with shape symbols, 70. *See also* Punctuation Indicator

Approximately equal to, 60

Arc, 75

Arrows, as signs of comparison, 68; as modifier, 75-77

At (@), 62

Bar, vertical: as grouping symbol, 48; as comparison symbol, 65; horizontal: under "inclusion," 65; as modifier, 75-76

Base Line Indicator, 71-74

Belongs to, 65

Boldface Type, 35

Borrowing, in subtraction problems, 22-25

Braces, 44-49, 65-66

Brackets, 44-49, 65-66

Cancellation, 21-25; indicators, 21; in reducing fractions, 21-22; in subtraction problems, 22-25; in addition or subtraction of mixed numbers, 23-24; rewriting in place of cancellation, 25

Cap (Intersection), 65-66

Capitalization, 40

Caret, in division, 11

Carried Numbers, 6-7

Cent Sign (¢), 62

Circle, 67, 69-70

Clock Time, 31-32

Comma, mathematical, 2, 26, 30; in multiplication problems, 8

Comparison Signs: equals, 4; others, 60-61; in set notation, 65; shapes as comparison signs, 67-68

Complex Fractions, 17-18

Computation, spatial arrangements for, 5-20; addition and subtraction, 5-6; multiplication, 7; multiplication with decimals, 8; division, 9-15; division with decimals, 10-14; using caret, 11; "serial subtraction," 12-14; remainders, 15; computation with fractions and mixed numbers, 19-20; involving cancellation, 21-25

Congruence, 60

Contained (Subset of), 65

Contracted Form of Right-Pointing Arrow, 68

Contracted Form of Horizontal Bar as Modifier, 76

Contractions, 50-59; use and non-use, general rules, 50-51; in fractions, 50; with function names, 52; in abbreviations, 52-53; in acronyms, 53; *to, into, by,* 54-55; in ordinal endings, 56; with grouping symbols, 57-58; resembling mathematical expressions, 58; with modifier symbols, 76; with radicals, 78; summary of rules, 84

Crosshatch (#), 64

Cube Root, 78

Cup (Union), 65-66

Dash (long): punctuation indicator with, 27, 29; spacing, 31; with adjacent hyphen, 31; as omission symbol, 33; contractions with, 55

Dash (normal), 31

Decimals, 3; multiplication with, 8; division with, 10-14; repeating, 76

Degree Sign, 74

Diagonal Line (Slash, /), 64

122 Index

Diagrams, English-Letter Indicator in, 39
Directly over, Directly under, 75. *See also* Modifiers
Ditto Marks, 63
Dividing a line. *See* Runover to New Line
Division: sign, 4; formats, 9-15; by "serial subtraction," 12-14
Dollar Sign ($), 62
Dot: multiplication, 4; as modifier, 75-76
Double Prime, 62

Element of (Member of), in sets, 65
Ellipsis: Punctuation Indicator with, 27, 29; spacing with, 31; as omission symbol, 33; as item in "enclosed list," 45; contractions with, 55
Empty Set, 65-66
Enclosed List, 44-45; defined, 44; Numeric Indicator in, 44; English-Letter Indicator in, 45; function names as items in, 45
English Braille, 1; use of numerals of, 2
English-Letter Indicator, 36-39; with "single letters" and "short-form combinations," 36-38; in fractions, 37; with plural, possessive, or ordinal endings, 38; with Roman numerals, 38; in diagrams and tables, 39; with abbreviations, 41-42; in "enclosed lists," 45; in other groupings, 46; with shapes, 70; summary of rules, 83
Enlarged Grouping Symbols, 48
Equals: sign, 4; not equal to, 60; greater than or equal to, 60; less than or equal to, 60; approximately equal to, 60; identically equal to, 60
Exponents, 71, 74

Feet, 41-43; prime representing feet, 62; *See also* Abbreviations
Five-Step Rule for Modified Expressions, 75
Format: for spatial arrangements, 5-20; Cancellation, 21; English-Letter Indicator in spatial fractions, 37; general rules, 79; runovers, 80-81

Fractions, 16-20; simple, 16; mixed numbers, 17, complex, 17; spatial arrangements, 18; addition and subtraction of, 19-20; cancellation in, 21; reducing of, 21-22; English-Letter Indicator in spatial arrangements of, 37
Function Names and Abbreviations: Punctuation Indicator following, 28; English-Letter Indicator with, 37; as items in "enclosed list," 45; contractions in, 52

General Omission Symbol, 33-34; Punctuation Indicator following, 33; contactions with, 50
Greater than, 60; or equal to, etc., 60
Greek-Letter Indicator, 36
Grouping Symbols, 44-49; symbols, 44; "enclosed list" defined, 44; Numeric Indicator with items in, 44-45; English-Letter Indicator with items in, 45-46; vertical bars as, 48; transcriber's grouping symbols, 48; enlarged symbols, 48; Punctuation Indicator following, 49; Empty Set, 65-66

Hexagon, 67-70
Horizontal Bar as modifier, 75-76
Hyphen, 3, 30; with adjacent dash, 31; Numeric Indicator following, 32

Identity (Identically Equal to), 60
If and Only If, 68
Inches, 41; and contractions, 53; double prime representing, 62
Inclusion (Contained in), 65
Index of Radical, 78
Indicators: general concept, 1; Greek letter, 36. *See also* English-Letter, Base-Line, Cancellation, Capitalization, Fraction, Modification, Multipurpose, Numeric, Punctuation, Radical, Shape, Superscript and Subscript
Infinite Number Line, 68
Intersection (Cap), 65-66

Index

Italics, influence on contractions within grouping symbols, 58; *See also* Type Forms

"Justifying," right and left, 11, 19

Less than, 60; negated, or equal to, 60
Letter Sign. *See* English-Letter Indicator
Level Indicators, 71-74
Line over, Line under, 75-77
Long Numerals, 2-3

Mathematical Expression, definition, 80
Measurements: abbreviations of, 41; contractions in, 52
Membership (Elements of), in sets, 65
Minus Sign, 4; minus numbers, Numeric Indicator with, 4
Minutes: abbreviation of, 52; of time and angle (Prime), 62
Miscellaneous Signs and Symbols, 62-64
Mixed Numbers, 17; addition and subtraction of, 19-20, 24-25
Modifiers, 75-77, five-step rule for formation, 75; contracted form, 76; recurring decimal digits, 76; contractions in modified expressions, 76
Multiplication: cross and dot, 4; spatial arrangements of, 7-8
Multipurpose Indicator, 15, 43, 63, 69, 72, 75; summary of rules, 85

Negation Sign, 60
Negative Numbers, 4
Not equal to, 60
Null Set (Empty Set), 65
Number Sign, 1. *See also* Numeric Indicator
Numerals, 1-2; in nondecimal bases, 3
Numeric Indicator: general use and non-use 1-4; after minus symbol, 4; in spatial arrangements for computation, 5; with fractions, 16, 18; with punctuation, 31-32 within grouping symbols, 44-45; summary of rules, 82

Numeric "Signs" and "Symbols," definitions, 1
Numeric Subscripts, 71-73

Octagon, 67-70
Omissions, 33-34, General Omission Symbol, 33; Punctuation Indicator following, 33; dash and ellipsis as omission symbols, 33; in spatial computations, 34; as items in "enclosed list," 45; shape symbols as omission indicators, 69
One-to-One Correspondence, 68
"Open" Numerals, 2
"Open" Number Line, 68
Operation Symbols, 4, 16; abbreviations with, 42; slash as, 64; intersection, 66; union, 66
Ordinal Endings: Punctuation Indicator following, 27; English-Letter Indicator with, 38; non-use of contractions in, 56

Page Numbering, 2
Parallel to, 67
Parentheses, 44-49
Per (Diagonal Line, /), 64
Percent, 62
Perpendicular to, 67
Pi, 36
Plural Endings: Punctuation Indicator with, 27; English-Letter Indicator with, 38; with shapes, 70
Pounds Symbol (#), 64
Powers (Exponents), 71-74
Prime, 62
Proportion, 60
Punctuation Indicator: general use and non-use, 26-31; following ordinal endings, 27; with plural and possessive endings, 27; following function names, 28; after general omission symbol, 33; after "single letters," 37; with abbreviations, 41; with grouping symbols, 49; after symbols of comparison, 61; after miscellaneous signs and symbols, 63;

Index

124

Punctuation Indicator: (Cont).
after shape symbols, 69; after modified expressions, 76; summary of rules, 82

Radicals, 78; index of, 78; contractions in, 78; spatial arrangements of, 78
Ratio, 60
Rectangle, 67-70
Recurring Decimal (Repeating Decimal), 76
Reference, abbreviations of, 42
Remainders, 15. *See also* Division
Reverse Inclusion (Contains), in sets, 65
"Right Justify," 11, 19
Roman Numerals: Punctuation Indicator following, 26; English-Letter Indicator with, 38; contractions with, 55
Runover to New Line, 3, 27, 45, 80-81

Sanserif Type, 35
Script Type, 35
Seconds, 62
Separation Line: in addition, subtraction, 5-6; in multiplication, 7; in division, 9-10
Set Brackets, 44-49, 65
Set Notation, 65-66
Shapes, 67-70; Indicator, 67; spacing with, 67; in "enclosed lists," 67; as omission symbols, 69; having mathematical significance, 69; plural of, 70; Multipurpose Indicator with, 69; English-Letter Indicator with, 70
Short-Form Combinations, 36-39
Since (Because ∵), 62
"Single Letter," 36-39. *See also* English-Letter Indicator
Slash (Diagonal line, /), 64
Spatial Arrangement: addition, 5; definition, 5; subtraction, 5; multiplication, 7; division, 9-15; fractions, 18
Spatial Formats, *See* Formats
Square, 67-70
Square Root, 78

Subscripts, 71-74; right numeric subscripts, 71-72; Punctuation Indicator following, 72; contractions in, 74
Subset, 65
"Subtractive Method" of Division, 12-14
Subtraction: minus sign, 4; of fractions and mixed numbers, 19, 24-25
Such That, 65
Superscripts, 71-74; Punctuation Indicator following, 72; contractions in, 74

Tables, English-Letter Indicator with letters in, 39
Tally Mark, 63
Therefore (∴), 62
Time (Clock), 32, 41; prime and double prime representing minutes and seconds, 62
Times Sign, 4; *See also* Multiplication
To, Into, By, contraction limitations, 54-55
Transcriber's Notes, 48. *See also* Grouping Symbols
Triangle, 67-70
Type Forms, 35

Union (Cup), 66

Vertical Bars: as grouping symbols, 48; "such that," 65

Weight, abbreviations of, 41
Word Contractions, literary. *See* Contractions